T0329037

Cambridge Elements ≡

Elements in the Politics of Development
edited by
Melani Cammett
Harvard University
Ben Ross Schneider
Massachusetts Institute of Technology

Series co-sponsored by

 MIT CENTER FOR INTERNATIONAL STUDIES

DEVELOPMENTAL STATES

Stephan Haggard
University of California San Diego

 CAMBRIDGE
UNIVERSITY PRESS

CAMBRIDGE
UNIVERSITY PRESS

University Printing House, Cambridge CB2 8BS, United Kingdom

One Liberty Plaza, 20th Floor, New York, NY 10006, USA

477 Williamstown Road, Port Melbourne, VIC 3207, Australia

314–321, 3rd Floor, Plot 3, Splendor Forum, Jasola District Centre,
New Delhi – 110025, India

79 Anson Road, #06–04/06, Singapore 079906

Cambridge University Press is part of the University of Cambridge.

It furthers the University's mission by disseminating knowledge in the pursuit of
education, learning, and research at the highest international levels of excellence.

www.cambridge.org
Information on this title: www.cambridge.org/9781108449496
DOI: 10.1017/9781108552738

© Stephan Haggard 2018

First published 2018

A catalogue record for this publication is available from the British Library.

ISBN 978-1-108-44949-6 Paperback
ISSN 2515-1584 (online)
ISSN 2515-1576 (print)

Cambridge Elements ☰

Developmental States

Stephan Haggard

Abstract: *The concept of the developmental state emerged to explain the rapid growth of a number of countries in East Asia in the postwar period. Yet the developmental state literature also offered a theoretical approach to growth that was heterodox with respect to prevailing approaches in both economics and political science. Arguing for the distinctive features of developmental states, its proponents emphasized the role of government intervention and industrial policy as well as the significance of strong states and particular social coalitions. This literature blossomed into a wider approach, firmly planted in a much longer heterodox tradition. Comparative analysis explored the East Asian developmental states to countries that were decidedly not developmentalist, thus contributing to our historical understanding of long-run growth. This Element provides a critical but sympathetic overview of this literature and ends with its revival and a look forward at the possibilities for developmentalist approaches, in both the advanced industrial states and developing world.*

Keywords: *East Asia; economic development, growth, industrial policy; state*

ISBNs: 9781108449496 (PB) 9781108552738 (OC)
ISSNs: 2515-1584 (online) 2515-1576 (print)

My thanks to Nancy Bermeo, Melanie Cammett, Miguel Centeno, Chonghyun Choi, Iza Ding, Dieter Ernst, Peter Gourevitch, Herbert Kitschelt, Jason Kuo, Jim Mahoney, Barry Naughton, T. J. Pempel, Seth Pipkin, Ben Schneider, Dan Slater, Barbara Stallings, Kathy Thelen, Robert Wade, David Waldner, Jong–sung You, and participants of a workshop at MIT in March 2017. Dani Rodrik and Peter Evans provided wise comments for the press. I wrote this while visiting the University of Pittsburgh; my thanks to Scott Mainwaring. Special thanks to Rick Doner, who helped me every step of the way.

1 Introduction

The concept of the developmental state entered the social science lexicon at quite a precise point in time: with the publication of Chalmers Johnson's *MITI and the Japanese Miracle* (1982).[1] This magisterial book was agenda-setting, and its insights were quickly extended to understand developments elsewhere in Asia. What might be called the "high" developmental state era encompassed the 1950s and 1960s in Japan and the 1960s and 1970s in Korea and Taiwan. Singapore and even apparently laissez-faire Hong Kong were included in these comparisons as well. Somewhat more cautiously, the concept was deployed to understand Southeast Asian cases such as Thailand and Malaysia in the 1970s and 1980s, although with some significant debate about whether they fit the developmental state model or not.

Yet as will be seen, the developmental state literature widens out in a variety of important ways: to a longer history of heterodox thinking about the role of the state in the development process; to comparisons between countries that grew rapidly and those that didn't; and ultimately to the economics and politics of growth itself. The developmental state concept challenged received wisdom about the appropriate policies for achieving rapid economic growth and the institutions – and politics – for getting there. As a result, the concept has seen a surprising revival. Even if the East Asian growth model appeared *sui generis*, could elements of it be replicated elsewhere? Could states learn to be "developmental" in at least some respects?

Initial proponents of the concept had two intellectual purposes. The first was to challenge orthodox explanations of economic development that focused primarily on market forces. They targeted an emergent body of neoclassical thinking that East Asia's

---

[1] For other reviews of the developmental state approach, see Öniş 1991; Henderson 1993, Moon and Prasad 1997; Leftwich 1995; Woo-Cumings 1999; Haggard 2004 and 2015; Routley 2012.

growth was caused by the adoption of market-conforming policies, most particularly with respect to the external sector. Johnson's central claim was that Japan's high postwar growth could be traced to industrial policies that differed from both the "plan ideological" systems of state socialism and the "regulatory state" of Anglo-Saxon capitalism. This branch of the research program focused on the relationship between economic policy and growth and attracted the broadest attention because it directly challenged liberal orthodoxy in the academy and development policy community. Led by intellectual outsiders – Chalmers Johnson, Alice Amsden (1989), Robert Wade (White and Wade 1984; Wade 1990/2004), and Ha-Joon Chang (1994) – this line of thinking was picked up by a number of sociologists (Appelebaum and Henderson 1992; Evans 1995) and subsequently adopted by economists with a heterodox bent (Rodrik 1995; Stiglitz 2001).

A second research agenda probed the *political* foundations of rapid growth. Industrial policy in the developing world was ubiquitous, but not ubiquitously successful. What was the political economy of successful industrial policy? And where did the institutions capable of conducting such policies come from in the first place? As with its economic face, the political theory of the developmental state also implicitly challenged an emerging orthodoxy. The developmental state literature took an institutionalist approach to politics, but not one focusing on the rule of law and property rights that characterized the so-called new institutionalist economics, nor on formal political institutions that preoccupied most political scientists. Rather, the initial emphasis was on the autonomy or insulation of the government from rent-seeking private interests, delegation to lead agencies, and coherent bureaucracies.

Johnson was also acutely aware of the centrality of business–government relations to the Japanese model, however. Subsequent contributions by Peter Evans (1989; 1995) and others refocused debate on the social foundations of rapid growth, and particularly the relationship between the state, the private sector, and labor organizations that appeared politically subordinated and tightly controlled.

In addition to these substantive contributions, the methodological approach of the developmental state literature was also distinctive. Components of the developmental state approach have been formalized, including those related to the idea of increasing returns and a variety of market failures and externalities. Efforts have been made to formalize the political economy of successful developmental states as well. There has also been a handful of efforts to test developmental state claims econometrically, either through cross-national quantitative designs or through studies of the effects of intervention on particular industries.

Yet much of the developmental state research agenda – as well as important progenitors – took a comparative historical approach that treated a small number of country and industry cases in great depth. Although Johnson offers a summary statement of the concept of the developmental state in the conclusion to *MITI* (315–324), he saw that effort largely as a characterization of the Japanese case, the elaboration of an historically grounded ideal type. He was cautious about generalization and explicitly warned that while "it may be possible for another state to adopt Japan's priorities and its high-growth system without duplicating Japan's history . . . the dangers of institutional abstraction are as great as the potential advantages" (307). Rather than seeking to isolate the influence of discrete causal variables, Johnson and his followers took an historical and configurational approach to explanation. They showed how some common features of these countries combined to promote economic growth, but left ample room for variation and nuance.

This method was closely related to theoretical priors. A strong theme in Johnson's book is that historical analysis was required because successful strategies only emerged through a process of trial and error and learning by doing that were always to some extent *sui generis*. Alice Amsden (2003), Dani Rodrik (2008), and Peter Evans (2010; Evans and Heller 2015) elevated these observations about learning into a virtual dictum about successful development more generally: that governments, societies, and firms need to learn and expand the capabilities of their citizens and workers in order to grow.

This short introduction to developmental states is divided into four main substantive sections and a brief conclusion. The first looks at progenitors and what Erik Reinert (2007) refers to as "the Other Canon." Although the developmental state concept emerged at a particular time, the underlying ideas associated with it have very much longer lineage. These approaches were grounded in the premise that industrialization in late developers differed fundamentally from the process in first movers, in large part because of the international context. Backwardness dictated that the state would play a quite different role in the growth process, substituting for the weakness of private institutions. Yet despite a number of commonalities in these approaches – foreshadowed in Alexander Gerschenkron's classic "Economic Backwardness in Historical Perspective" – a distinct Japanese tradition of thinking about late development bears close scrutiny as well. Akamatsu Kaname's flying geese theory shared some commonalities with developmentalist thinking elsewhere in the postwar world, but differed in the emphasis it placed on industrializing through exports.

Section 3 looks more closely at the relationship between intervention and growth, considering both Johnson's contribution and the analysis of the other paradigmatic East Asian cases. This discussion situates the developmental state literature in the context of the neoclassical revival in development economics, itself spurred by analysis of the newly industrializing countries of East Asia. An overarching theoretical theme is the idea that growth is hampered by a range of market failures and coordination problems that are only overcome through state action: in moving into new industrial activities, in financial market failures, and in questions surrounding technology transfer, adoption, and learning. A review of some exemplary cases shows clearly that these interventions need to be understood not simply in terms of policies undertaken by a welfare-maximizing state but in terms of institutions that elicited information and permitted coordination between the state and private sector.

Section 4 considers the political economy of developmental states, including the question of their origins. As noted, the developmental states implicitly challenged an existing orthodoxy in political economy. In contrast to the property rights and "rule of law" approach, the developmental state literature emphasized strong – and even authoritarian – executives and coherent, merito-cratic, or "Weberian" bureaucracies. Proponents of the develop-mental state approach gradually widened their purview from institutional factors to the social underpinnings of growth in the close but controlled relations between the state and the private sector and the subordination of labor. These strands of work on the social foundations of the developmental state culminated in a deep historical discussion of origins, including comparisons with states that were decidedly not "developmental." An important feature of this literature was a focus on international context, particularly in providing mechanisms that constrained potentially predatory state elites.

Section 5 looks forward and considers the apparent decline and subsequent rebirth of the developmental state concept. A number of developments in the late twentieth century seemed to funda-mentally undercut the classic developmental state model. The first was international. The high-growth Asian countries emerged at a propitious moment, tied by alliances to an American hegemon that was leading a liberalization of the world economy on which they could free ride. Yet the very success of these latecomers triggered the so-called new protectionism and internal as well as external pressures forced them to gradually liberalize. Political change also appeared to undercut the classic developmental state approach. Democratization called into question the auton-omy of the state and the close business–government alliances and subordination of labor that constituted the social underpinnings of the model.

Yet developmentalist ideas proved resilient and adaptive, and in the second decade of the twenty-first century the developmental state witnessed a surprising revival. The neoliberal moment of the immediate post–Cold War period did not prove enduring, particu-larly in the wake of the global financial crisis of 2008. Across the developing world, concerns about premature deindustrialization and broader middle-income traps led to a quest for a new, open-economy industrial policy. The rapid growth of China, Vietnam, and India appeared to usher in a new generation of heterodox success cases. Nor did political change dampen the demand for developmentalist thinking. To the contrary, democratization generated a quest for new growth strategies, and a wide-ranging debate ensued about what a "democratic developmental state" might look like.

In the concluding section, I summarize the enduring contribution of the developmental state approach. The tradition is very much alive because it reflects a persistent, contested, and unresolved debate about the appropriate relationship among states, publics, and markets in the growth process. It is also alive because it reflects a way of thinking about development that retains methodological appeal, namely an approach grounded in comparative historical analysis and an acknowledgment of the enduring variety of capitalist systems.

2 Progenitors and Parallels: The Heterodox Lineage

Although the developmental state literature emerged to explain a very particular problem – the rapid growth of Japan and the newly industrializing countries of Asia – the ideas undergirding the concept have a much longer lineage, and one that is likely to persist. This tradition constitutes an alternative approach to economic growth that is self-consciously opposed to dominant liberal models and favorably disposed to state intervention: in mobilizing savings and investment and in influencing the sectoral allocation of resources through planning, trade, and industrial policies, and strategic use of the financial system.

When did this alternative canon first appear? Some, including particularly Reinert (2007), reach back to very early examples of state support for manufacturing by Europe's absolutist monarchs. However, these appear tied largely to prestige projects and were not linked to what we would now call a growth strategy. Nor is the classic mercantilist system – roughly from 1650 to 1780 – described in such rich detail by Hecksher (1931/1994) – relevant. Early mercantilism referred to the economic-cum-political systems of competing great powers, not latecomers, and predated the spread of the Industrial Revolution and the particular forms of international specialization that accompanied it.

We only see the emergence of developmentalist ideas and practice as defined here in the period of British dominance of the world economy – from the onset of the Industrial Revolution through World War I – and in the interwar period and subsequent rise of American hegemony. Advocacy of support for industry in the context of an emerging international division of labor can be seen quite clearly in Alexander Hamilton's remarkable *Report on Manufactures* (1791/1892) and on the continent in a tradition of German political economy running from Friedrich List's (1841) *National System of Political Economy* to the work of Gustav Schmoller (1884/1902), among others. The problematic was theorized with particular clarity by Gerschenkron (1962) in his essay on "Economic Backwardness in Historical Perspective," which raises many of the fundamental political as well economic issues of late industrialization. Since Gerschenkron is frequently invoked in developmental state work, the essay deserves careful dissection.

2.1 Gerschenkron on Late Development: The Nineteenth-Century European Experience

In the preface to *Das Kapital*, Marx defends his focus on England by stating boldly that "the country that is more developed industrially only shows, to the less developed, the image of its own future." Gerschenkron (1962) begged to differ. Industrialization in backward countries and regions "showed considerable differences ... not only with regard to the speed of development but also with regard to the productive and organizational structures of industry which emerge from those processes" (7).

Gerschenkron followed Veblen's intuitions about the critical role of technology transfer in late industrialization, including with respect to Japan (1915a) and Germany (1915b). He argues that the larger the backlog of technologies that can be absorbed from the industrial leaders, the greater the opportunities for industrialization.[2] Yet many activities based on these technologies, most notably iron and steel production, are characterized by significant economies of scale. Gerschenkron also notes the imperative for latecomers of initiating many lines of economic activity at once due to the existence of complementarities and indivisibilities among them. Moving manufactured goods to market requires railroads, railroads require steel, steel requires coal, and so on. Missing linkages do not simply impose costs; they threaten the entire industrial enterprise.

If "catching up" places particular demands on follower countries, the question turns to the institutions required for overcoming particular barriers to growth: absorbing technologies, realizing economies of scale, and exploiting externalities. Unlike other progenitors – including Hamilton, List, and postwar heterodox accounts – Gerschenkron did not see protectionism as a central feature of European catch-up. Yet he argues that in the absence of industrial banking institutions such as Credit Mobilier in France, capital would not have been mobilized and takeoff would not have occurred. Drawing on the German case, he sees the evolution of distinctive systems of bank–industry relationships – in effect, varieties of capitalism to use a later moniker (Hall and Soskice 2001) – as a direct result of the imperatives of backwardness.

What about the role of the state? Gerschenkron is often misread on this point, as he does not see a strong interventionist state role in the more immediate followers such as Italy, Switzerland, or France. Rather, Gerschenkron argues that the extent of state intervention is correlated with the degree of backwardness. He uses a natural experiment between the more- and less-developed western and eastern parts of the Austro-Hungarian empire to make the point and puts particular emphasis on the Russian case. The banking

---

[2] He also explicitly notes that low wages are *not* an advantage since they typically reflect the predominance of rural employment and inadequate skills; Amsden (1991) returns to this point as well.

revolution and new forms of bank–industry relations that drove industrialization in the early followers did not emerge in Russia, nor could they have. In an example of the functionalist logic visible in some strands of the developmental state literature as well, Gerschenkron argues that the task of forcing and financing industrialization fell more centrally to the state as a result. Gerschenkron claims that preferential orders to domestic producers of railway materials, and subsidies, credits, and profit guarantees to new industrial enterprises were all central to the spurt of industrial growth Russia experienced up until the revolution.

It is hard to overstate the prescience of the Gerschenkron essay vis-à-vis the subsequent developmental state literature: the most basic idea that industrialization is crucial to catch-up; that development strategies must be seen in an international context; that specialization might be inimical to growth; that technology, increasing returns, and externalities are central features of industrialization; that capitalism is not of a single piece but shows important variation in latecomers; and that institutions – including the state – play crucial roles in the growth process.

But in one important regard noted, Gerschenkron is at variance with the heterodox canon, and that is in his failure to consider how the international economic context shapes the interests of latecomers, and with respect to trade policy in particular. In his *Report on Manufacturers* (1791/1892), Hamilton foreshadows later heterodox arguments by arguing for protection as an instrument for avoiding an unfavorable position in the international division of labor.[3] But Hamilton went farther: he argued that the first movers *themselves* had benefited from "bounties, premiums

---

[3] Were the world system characterized by free trade, Hamilton argued, promotion of manufactures would not be necessary and countries would gravitate toward their "natural" comparative advantage. But the United States in fact faced "numerous and very injurious impediments to the emission and vent of their own commodities. In such a position of things, the United States cannot exchange with Europe on equal terms; and the want of reciprocity would render them the victim of a system which would induce them to confine their views to agriculture and refrain from manufactures" (24).

and other aids," and had subsequently misrepresented their own economic history.

The hypocrisy of early industrializers resurfaces strongly among heterodox accounts of the European growth experience, including among those tied directly to the developmental state tradition. Noteworthy in this regard is the work of economic historian Paul Bairoch (1972, 1995) and particularly Ha-Joon Chang (2002). In a typically contrarian piece written in 1972, Bairoch argues that the effects of free trade and protection had diametrically opposite effects in Britain on the one hand and France, Germany, and Italy on the other. In the leading economy, liberalization accelerated growth; in the latecomers, it had adverse effects on output, innovation, and investment that were only reversed with the reimposition of tariffs.[4] In a contribution geared directly to the industrial policy debate, Chang's *Kicking Away the Ladder* (2002) follows Bairoch explicitly, concluding that the Anglo-American orthodoxy advocating free trade does not match the historical record of how the rich countries got rich over the course of the nineteenth century. Rather, Chang argues, these claims reflected an effort to "kick away the ladder," denying the opportunities first movers had enjoyed to their potential challengers.

2.2 Postwar Progenitors

Not surprisingly, these arguments were replayed both among theorists and practitioners in the postwar period. In a sweeping but nonetheless useful generalization, Findlay and O'Rourke (2007, 488–489) note that during the late nineteenth century, "European powers imposed free trade policies on much of Africa and Asia, while retaining protectionist barriers themselves (the outstanding exception being the free trade–trading United

---

[4] It should be noted that the mechanism generating these effects comports with developmental state ideas somewhat indirectly. Bairoch argued that the slow-down in growth was associated with the fall in rural demand as a result of the integration of grain markets; protection revived rural incomes as well as urban ones, generating domestic demand.

Kingdom)."[5] In the summary statement of her ideas, *The Rise of "the Rest"* (2001, 31–98), Amsden details how such integration devastated indigenous industry in a number of latecomers, including Turkey and India, and set back the early learning that she believed was important for subsequent industrialization.

During the early decades of the postwar period, this pattern would reverse. The North Atlantic economy revived around a program of gradual liberalization among the advanced industrial states while developing countries experimented with statist and inward-looking policies. These ideas played out in somewhat different ways in Latin America, the Middle East, and South Asia, as Amsden (2001, 99–189) shows. But as in nineteenth-century America and continental Europe, important strands of thinking bear a family resemblance to the longer-standing heterodox canon.[6]

The disadvantages of the prevailing international division of labor were paramount in early postwar development thinking. Among the more influential stylized facts in this regard were the observations of Paul Singer (1950) and Raul Prebisch (1950) about the secular decline in the terms of trade between commodities and manufactures and the need for import-substituting strategies. These strategies subsequently became the *bête noire* of the neoclassical revival.

Yet a careful reading of Prebisch's initial manifesto suggests a very much wider agenda than enfant industry protection, as well as cognizance of the political risks of *dirigism*. Prebisch certainly agreed with the underlying premise in all developmentalist thinking that industrialization was the key to long-run growth: through its influence on productivity growth, capital accumulation, and the generation of employment. As simple as this idea may seem, it too required defense. This defense was forthcoming in the postwar period through Keynesian contributions to the theory of

---

[5] In a well-known treatment, Gallagher and Robinson (1953) characterize this phenomenon as "the imperialism of free trade."

[6] I set aside here the complex question of the influence of Soviet ideas on developing countries given that they represented an altogether different model than the mixed economy approach of interest here.

economic growth and their extension to developing countries. Prominent in this lineage were the Harrod-Domar growth model, with its emphasis on capital accumulation and investment (Harrod 1939; Domar 1946). But particularly important were the "big push" approach of Ragnar Nurkse (Kattel, Kregel, and Reinert 2009) and Paul Rosenstein-Rodan (1943), the latter of which drew directly on Eastern European experience, and Albert Hirschman's (1958) concept of "unbalanced" growth, with its emphasis on externalities associated with intersectoral linkages. Nicholas Kaldor's (1957, 1967) famous "laws" linking manufacturing growth both to overall economic growth and productivity growth became a heterodox touchstone as well.

As the Keynesian lineage of these early development economists would suggest, growth was seen as requiring a strong state role and even planning processes to mobilize resources and allocate them in ways that were dynamically efficient. Increasing returns, in the broadest sense, played a central theoretical role. Among those working on the developmental state, Amsden (2001) put the most emphasis on the gains from these early developmentalist efforts, arguing that import-substituting activities were crucial for learning in the small group of countries that subsequently accounted for the bulk of the developing world's industrial output. As we will see, the neoclassical revival reached exactly opposite conclusions, seeing in interventionist policies little more than a fundamental drag on growth.

It is also important to emphasize that the approach to trade-cum-industrial policy in the developmentalist canon, including Prebisch, was more attuned to risks than is often thought. Prebisch shared a widespread export pessimism, but he was quite clear about the risks of protectionist policies as well, raising an important political economy point that was to become central to the developmental state literature. "If industrialization is considered to be the means of attaining an autarchic ideal in which economic considerations are of secondary importance," Preibisch wrote (1950, 6), "any industry that can produce substitutes for imports is justifiable. If, however, the aim is to increase the measurable well-being of the masses, the limits beyond which more intensive industrialization might mean a decrease in productivity must be borne in mind." An important conclusion follows: whatever supportive or protective measures the state might pursue to achieve the benefits of industrialization had to be matched by the capacity to weed out the claims of the inefficient.[7]

It is again beyond the scope of this introduction to replay these lines of thought in other regions; Latin America is chosen because of the stylized comparisons between the East Asian and Latin American cases that subsequently became a staple of both neo-classical and developmental state accounts (particularly Gereffi and Wyman 1990; Haggard 1990; Evans 1995). But the brief treatment here does underscore the common theme that catch-up requires a focus on industrialization and that objective is not likely to be achieved in the absence of state intervention and protection.

2.3   Asian Alternatives: The Flying Geese Model

Which brings me to the last and arguably most relevant precursor to the developmental state idea: the concept of the flying geese model of industrialization.[8] The flying geese model appears to bear a number of similarities to developmentalist ideas elsewhere in placing the problematic of late development in an international context, in putting its focus on industrialization as the key to growth, and in noting the crucial role of state steering and even of well-timed protectionist measures. Yet this highly influential strand of Japanese thinking differed from those of the Keynesians and developmentalists elsewhere in embracing international specialization as a path to industrial growth.

---

[7] Nor were the limits of import substitution ignored by the broader movement of *desarollismo* in Latin America, including by its primary intellectual proponents in CEPAL, the highly influential Economic Commission for Latin America and the Caribbean (Kay 1989, 36–46). As early as the 1960s, little more than a decade following Prebisch's initial broadside, CEPAL as well as structuralist critics on the left were already noting the "exhaustion" of ISI. One result was a new push for regional integration that would expand trade opportunities and permit greater intraregional specialization.

[8] Curiously, Johnson makes no mention of Akamatsu or this lineage of thinking.

We do not yet have a thorough study of the intellectual influence that the flying geese model had on Asian countries outside Japan. But the fact that these ideas were developed within Asia and so clearly matched the actual experience of a country that had "taken off" is of obvious relevance to their diffusion. This point was made most strongly by Bruce Cumings (1984) in his essay "The Origins and Development of the Northeast Asian Political Economy." It was later picked up by a number of other analysts as well, although sometimes critically (Bernard and Ravenhill 1995).

Akamatsu Kaname's flying geese theory was developed over the course of the 1930s and subsequently underwent ongoing modification and clarification both by him and his followers well into the postwar period; the literature on it is now vast (see Korhonen 1994 and Kojima 2000 for reviews). Indeed, as we will see in recent debates about Chinese industrial policy, the flying geese model remains a focus of controversy to this day.

Akamatsu was initially doing little more than providing a descriptive account of Japan's industrialization vis-à-vis the European and American leaders. As with other proponents of the heterodox canon, Akamatsu (1962) begins the most widely read English-language version of the theory by noting in the very first sentence that "it is impossible to study the economic growth of the developing countries in modern times without considering the mutual interactions between these economies and those of the advanced countries" (3).[9]

Yet Akematsu's theory is ultimately one of complementarity and had two variants. The first traced the evolution of a given *industry* from leaders to followers and was in effect a theory of the diffusion of industrialization. The second mapped the gradual diversification and upgrading of industrial structure within a given follower:

---

[9] As Akamatsu notes, in many cases these relations were imperial and forced an unfavorable division of labor on developing countries. According to Korhonen (1994), Akamatsu's ideas were tainted in the eyes of some by the fact that they appeared to justify the imperial division of labor of Japan's Greater East Asia Co-Prosperity Sphere.

from basic consumer products through more capital- and technology-intensive activities.

In both variants, the import of manufactures from the leaders begins a process of "communication" that ultimately permits the follower countries to exploit a variety of advantages in emulating the leaders. These advantages include the existence of home markets – which Akamatsu believed in proto-Keynesian fashion must be adequate to foster growth – low wages, and locally available raw materials. These interactions are subsequently deepened as the leader countries export capital goods and intermediates that become crucial inputs to the import-substitution process. But the theory rests on the expectation that the development of local industry will be followed by manufactured *exports* back to the leader, which in turn forces the structural adjustments that push the leader into new activities. In a clever formulation, Terutomo Ozawa (1993, 2009) called this process "comparative advantage recycling."

In the postwar period, followers of Akamatsu (Kojima 1966; Okita 1985) reframed the flying geese model in a wider regional framework. Japanese development, trade, investment, and aid, according to Okita and others, would support regional integration and even explicit coordination of the flying geese process.

However, the role that the state played in the process has become the subject not only of controversy but selective memory. In the postwar period, Akamatsu's model was given a theoretical underpinning by Kojima (1966 2000) that looks surprisingly orthodox in formulation: invoking a standard Hecksher-Ohlin setup, linking the process of industrial spread to foreign direct investment (FDI) following Vernon (1966; see also Ozawa 1993), and eliding the issue of industrial policy almost altogether. Yet this formulation does not match what Akamatsu himself said. Akamatsu clearly believed that within any given country, difficult decisions would need to be made about steering resources toward "sunrise" industries and away from "sunset" ones; thus the link to industrial policy and to the developmental state that others later drew quite explicitly (for example, Kasahara 2013).

This brief review of "precursors and parallels" is not designed as an intellectual history or prehistory of the developmental state concept. The point is broader. All of the major proponents of the developmental state – and particularly Amsden – noted that the problematic of late development has a long lineage. These ideas include in the first instance the centrality of industrialization to growth and learning and the fact that laissez-faire policies might be inappropriate for latecomers.

Yet on one crucial issue we see nuanced internal disagreements among these latecomer theories, with some advocating virtually autarkic policies and others grappling with the risks of rent-seeking. In this regard, the flying geese model stands out as a quite distinctive way of thinking about late development, one in which the state has an important role but in the context of an export-oriented strategy. The power of this model was not simply intellectual: it gained force precisely because it conformed so clearly and closely to a successful follower, namely Japan. It is to how the developmental state "worked" that I now turn.

3 Sources of Growth: Industrial Policy in the Developmental States

As in our discussion of the heterodox canon more generally, the developmental state literature posed itself as an alternative to an emerging neoclassical consensus in development economics. Prior to the appearance of Johnson's (1982) book, a succession of highly influential studies by Little, Skitovsky, and Scott (1970), Krueger (1978) and Bhagwati (1978), and Balassa (1981) offered up a classic liberal interpretation of economic growth, relying heavily on the success of East Asian cases to make the argument. This work emphasized the significance of stable macroeconomic policies and the importance of other complementary market-oriented reforms. But trade and exchange rate policies were clearly the central focus. In dialectical fashion, this new orthodoxy was aimed directly at the body of postwar development thinking outlined in Section 2.

The grounds on which trade liberalization – broadly conceived – would lead not only to a one-off increase in the growth rate but a higher equilibrium growth path are by no means obvious. In the standard neoclassical growth model by Solow (1956), the sources of economic growth are to be found in the growth in inputs to production (capital, labor, and land), improvements in the efficiency of allocation of inputs across activities, and innovation of altogether new products and processes. The latter is typically identified with technological change and increases in the productivity of inputs (and treated as a residual to the growth accounting based on the role of factor inputs).[10] To the extent that the drivers of such models are exogenously determined increases in factor inputs, neoclassical models had the perverse implication that policy should have no effect on the steady-state rate of growth.

Yet as Bhagwati and Srinivasan (2001) argue in their spirited defense of the neoclassical interpretation, greater openness to trade can have effects on all components of the standard model, from increasing inputs to improving allocative efficiency and innovation. This is particularly true where the assumption is dropped that the marginal return to capital ineluctably trends toward zero, a point that was emphasized – ironically – in the Keynesian progenitors as well.

The force of this work did not rest on new theory, however. Nor did it attempt cross-national empirical modeling, as an outpouring of econometric studies on the trade–growth relationship did over the 1980s with somewhat mixed results (see Edwards 1993 for a review of the contemporaneous generation of such studies, and see Rodrik and Rodriguez 1999 for an influential critique). Rather, the influence of this early work came from detailed case studies of liberalization episodes. These included an early assessment of the experience of Korea and Taiwan by Little, Skitovsky, and Scott (1970) and a succession of studies of the East Asian

---

[10] These theories returned to the discussion on East Asia in a second generation of work that reinterpreted the growth of the developmental states as led by investment rather than exports; we take up this issue Section 3.2 and in Section 4 as well.

newly industrializing countries – including Hong Kong and Singapore – by Balassa (1981), Hughes (1988), and a myriad of others over the course of the 1970s and 1980s. In the ten-volume Bhagwati-Krueger project, cases included Chile, Colombia, Egypt, India, the Philippines, and Turkey, but Korea once again played a particularly important role.

In these studies, trade and exchange rate policy reforms appeared to have both macroeconomic (Krueger 1978, 268–274) and microeconomic consequences (Krueger 1978, 246–268): increasing exports, alleviating balance-of-payments constraints, and eliminating a myriad of distortions and inefficiencies in product and factor markets. Above all, reform episodes were followed not only by an expansion of trade but transitions to higher growth as well.

The implications of this advocacy of what came to be known – somewhat misleadingly – as "export-led growth" are hard to overestimate. The new orthodoxy about liberalization provided the key empirical referent for what economist John Williamson in 1989 called "the Washington consensus": a condensed checklist of ten policy reforms that gained currency as a result of the conservative turn in the major advanced industrial states marked by the elections of Margaret Thatcher (1979), Ronald Reagan (1980) and Helmut Kohl (1982). Given the larger political climate, neoclassical prescriptions moved quickly and seamlessly from academia into the development policy community and the international financial institutions.[11]

3.1 *Johnson's* MITI and the Japanese Miracle

Written a decade prior to the collapse of the Soviet Union, *MITI and the Japanese Miracle* was not responding directly to these

---

[11] When the World Bank (1993) finally did its own review of the East Asian miracle – at Japan's urging – the report downplayed the role of industrial policy, setting off a heated debate over both the substance of the report and the process through which it was written (Amsden 1994; Wade 1996; Aoki, Kim, and Okuno-Fujiwara 1996).

developments in the economics profession, although Johnson's followers decidedly were. But Johnson *was* responding to an earlier version of this debate about Japan.[12] Economists such as Patrick and Rosovsky (1976) played the orthodox foil, and Johnson took sharp aim at their interpretations in his introduction. He framed *MITI and the Japanese Miracle* in terms of a distinction between the plan-ideological systems of state socialism and two varieties of contemporary capitalism: market-rational and plan-rational systems. The fundamental difference between the latter two was that market-rational economies took a regulatory approach to economic activity while the plan-rational or developmental state was purposive and goal-directed. The developmental state sought to achieve high growth not through an arm's-length or parametric approach to policy but by influencing the allocation of resources to designated economic activities, a process subsequently known as "targeted" industrial policy.[13]

In a later reflection on the book, Johnson (1999, 56–58) agrees with a critic that the precise meaning of state leadership requires caution. He notes that Japan went through a progression of several distinct institutional and policy configurations. Self- or private control referred to a set of arrangements in which the state allows and even organizes private cartels; he sees this system prevailing through the 1930s when Japanese *zaibatsu* appeared to reign supreme. More direct state control followed during the war and in its immediate aftermath with the "imposition of state institutions onto the private economy, displacing private cartels, private

---

[12] Johnson (1999) himself reflects on the "odyssey" of the developmental state; the following paragraphs draws not only on his book but on that reflection. See also Johnson 1995. Johnson of course was not alone in seeing the role of the state and business–government relations as pivotal. See for example Lockwood (1954) and the body of work by Ronald Dore culminating in his *Flexible Rigidities* (1986). On the role of the business–government alliance on the politics of growth, see Pempel (1978).

[13] Throughout its life, the developmental state literature has been accused of tautology: that developmental states were little more than those that grew rapidly. But Johnson was rightly cautious on this point, arguing that whether such efforts were successful is not assumed.

ownership, private labor organizations with so-called control associations (*toseikei*) during the war and public corporations during the occupation and after" (see also Johnson 1978).

The equilibrium for the postwar period was neither of these systems but rather what he calls "cooperative management schemes" between the public and private sector. As we will see, this theme of coordination is a consistent one in the developmental state literature that followed. But it also became an ongoing point of contention in the analysis of Japan, as Johnson's challengers sought to place more weight on the role of the private sector and politicians.[14]

The core empirical finding of the book is that Japanese planners came to believe, through trial and error, that economic development required both "industrial rationalization" and "industrial structure" policies (27). The former referred to measures designed to solve problems of backwardness at the firm level: rationalizing enterprises and the environments they faced, but also rationalizing whole industries through "the creation of a framework for all enterprises in an industry in which each can compete fairly or in which they can cooperate in a cartellike arrangement of mutual assistance" (27).

The truly distinctive feature of the Japanese miracle, however, were MITI's "industrial structure" policies, which sought to actively change the *composition* of investment and output by targeting particular sectors along a dynamically efficient frontier. A central point of the book is that these policies were not a postwar

---

[14] Virtually anyone writing on the political economy of Japan in the two decades following Johnson was responding to his book in one way or the other. I take up the politics of the developmental state in Section 4, but among those that were cautious about the role of industrial policy are Samuels' (1987) study of energy markets; Friedman's (1988) study of the machine tool industry, with its emphasis on the growth of flexible manufacturing strategies among smaller firms; and Calder's (1993) emphasis on the role of financial institutions in Japanese growth. Studies of MITI's involvement in high-tech industries that extended but modified the MITI-led model included Okimoto's (1989) *Between MITI and the Market*, Anchourdougy's (1989) study of the computer industry, and Noble's (1998) comparative study of Japan and Taiwan.

phenomenon, but had their origins in indigenous Keynesian efforts – prior to Keynes' *General Theory* – to pull Japan out of the depression. These became evident according to Johnson as early as the second half of the 1920s. The initial ideas evolved through a complex process of learning by doing (103–105) and – quite controversially – were stamped powerfully by Japanese militarism; indeed, MITI's immediate predecessor was none other than the Ministry of Munitions.

Wartime controls provided the postwar planners with an unusual array of instruments for influencing industry, despite the American occupation: "control over all foreign exchange and imports of technology, which gave them the power to choose industries for development; the ability to dispense preferential financing, tax breaks, and protection from foreign competition, which gave them the power to lower the costs of the chosen industries; and the authority to order the creation of cartels and bank-based industrial conglomerates ... which gave them the power to supervise competition" (199). In addition, Johnson details the concept of "administrative guidance" (265–266). Johnson argues that bureaucratic dirigisme played a central role in industrial structure policies into the 1970s and was even of significance with respect to Japan's move into more technology-intensive industries (see also Okimoto 1989; Anchourdougy 1989; Noble 1998; Pekkanen 2003).

Johnson was not an economist and was cautious in making causal claims with respect to industrial policy. When he summarized the four crucial components of the developmental state model at the end of the book – and only then at the insistence of his editor (Johnson 1999, 39) – "market-conforming methods of state intervention" was third on the list. The other elements were all political: an elite state bureaucracy, a pilot agency like MITI, and a political system capable of delegating to these entities. It is also worth underscoring that although Johnson's book is associated with industrial policy, it does not generally descend to the level of particular industries, focusing much more centrally on the plans – the intentions – of the bureaucracy.[15] Rather, Johnson's method was to show in extraordinary detail what the Japanese planners were actually doing and why, with a particular focus on the organizational evolution of MITI and its pursuit of industrial policy. It was simply self-evident to Johnson that the structural changes that took place in Japan during the 1950s and the long boom of the 1960s – "the operative mechanism of the economic miracle" (31) – were causally related to what the state was doing.

3.2 Theory and Method in the Analysis of Industrial Policy

In contrast to Johnson's study, Wade's analysis of Taiwan, *Governing the Market: Economic Theory and the Role of Government in East Asian Industrialization* (1990, 2nd edition 2004), and the studies of Korea by Amsden (*Asian's Next Giant*, 1989) and Chang (*The Political Economy of Industrial Policy*, 1994) were more frontally engaged with the neoclassical canon on East Asian growth. As a result, they were more preoccupied with identifying the causal links between policy choices and growth than they were with the evolution and consequences of political and bureaucratic institutions.

Wade can be taken as a general introduction to the main themes, although the three books differed in important points of emphasis.[16] What Wade called the "governed market" or GM theory "emphasizes capital accumulation as the principal general force for growth, and interprets superior East Asian performance

---

[15] At one point early in the book, Johnson goes so far as to say that he could not "prove that a particular Japanese industry would not or could not have grown and developed at all without the government's industrial policy" (30) leaving that task to others. Industry analysis features much more prominently in a succession of studies of Japan that followed in his wake and sought to confirm, modify, or overturn altogether the central role of MITI and the state more generally.

[16] For example, Amsden was more preoccupied with the problem of technology transfer and learning; Chang was more intent on engaging prevailing theoretical literature on the role of the state.

as the result of a *level* and *composition* of investment different from what FM [free market] ... policies would have produced, and different, too, from what the 'interventionist' economic policies pursued by many other LDCs would have produced" (29, emphasis added).

Wade thus suggested that the existence of strong, developmental states helps explain the mobilization of savings and investment that undergirded all of the East Asian miracles. The theory was thus at least partially consistent with a line of argument that capital accumulation – rather than either liberalizing reforms or industrial policies – was at the core of the East Asian miracle. Grounded in studies by Kim and Lau (1994) and Young (1992; 1995), this approach was popularized by Krugman's (1994) widely read essay "The Myth of Asia's Miracle." Rather than a miracle, East Asia got high growth from exactly what Solow-style growth models predicted: that growth was a function of inputs, and by the growth in the capital stock in particular.

But sheer accumulation was clearly not at the heart of the developmental state story, which rested more fundamentally on the *allocation* of resources and state action to address market failures (Wade, 1990, 11–14, 350–58; Amsden 2001 139–155). Chang (1994, 61–78), more than any of the other theorists of the developmental state, sought to align the developmental state approach with the new institutional economics.[17] Chang justified state intervention on straightforward market failure grounds. But he also argued that informational asymmetries and transaction costs hindered the ability of governments to reach efficient policy decisions. As a result, the state had to effectively organize decision making in the presence of multiple agents with potentially conflicting interests and information. Institutions mattered for solving these problems, most notably consultative mechanisms between the state and the private sector. But Chang argued that the state could

---

[17] A full discussion of the new institutional economics is beyond the scope of this essay, but as we will see, it comes up in a second generation of cognate work. See, for example, Doner 2009, 64–94.

achieve these objectives not only by organizing its relations with private actors but by organizing the actors themselves, by serving as a focal point for private expectations and even through ideology or values around which expectations could converge (Chang 1994, 52–53).

Before turning to the precise nature of those coordination problems and some examples from canonical cases, it is important to say something about method. A surprisingly common research design in the literature on industrial policy is to pick a successful (or unsuccessful) industry, demonstrate that policy support existed, and conclude that the case for the significance of industrial policy is made (or rejected). Such an approach is hardly satisfying, suffering from quite obvious selection problems.

It would seem that a more standard approach would be readily available: to examine industry-level data within a given country to determine if those that received policy support surpassed those that did not on some metric, such as total factor productivity (TFP), exports, or profitability. The World Bank *Miracle* report (1993) purports to conduct some tests along these lines, although they are hard to follow (Amsden 1994). Lee (1996) provides another often-cited example of such econometric work, and Noland and Pack (2003) and Pack and Saggi (2006) both draw broadly skeptical conclusions about state intervention from the surprisingly small number of econometric studies in this vein.

Yet as Wade (2004, 29–33, 71–72, 109) points out, the task is much harder than it appears and requires a more complex counterfactual method. First, sector-specific policies must not only be plausibly associated with the success of the industry in question but must yield outcomes equal or superior to a more market-conforming policy counterfactual. Moreover, Wade goes farther by arguing that intervention must not be the result of private sector demands (what Wade calls "followership"); if they were, then the investments in question might have taken place anyway. Rather, intervention must reflect "leadership" by the state that puts the industrial structure or a particular industry on a different path than it would have otherwise taken.

Rodrik (2007) outlines clearly why standard econometric efforts do not escape the fundamental dilemmas of the counterfactual analysis undertaken by Wade:

> The almost insurmountable flaw in this [econometric] literature is that the key estimated coefficient [on industrial policy] ... cannot discriminate between two radically different views of the world: (a) the government uses industrial policy for political or other inappropriate ends, and its support ends up going to losers rather than winners; (b) the government optimally targets the sectors that are the most deserving of support, and does its job as well as it possibly can in a second-best policy environment. Under (a) governments should commit to a hands-off policy. Under (b) a hands-off approach would leave the economy worse off ... The empirical analysis leaves us no better informed than when we started. (17–18)

Other reviews also admit as much (Pack and Saggi 2006).

These problems help account for why much of the developmental state literature – including Johnson – has taken a macrocomparative historical form by looking at growth trajectories at the national level. Why did Japan, Korea, and Taiwan grow so rapidly? To what extent did reforms such as those isolated in the neoclassical account as opposed to industrial policies of various sorts help account for the timing of observed growth accelerations? What role did institutional reforms play in these processes?

Yet given the focus on particular coordination problems, the developmental state literature has always had an affinity with analysis at the industry level, where we can observe not only the operation of policy but also the institutional and political context in which it works. A failing of neoclassical interpretations was that they did not provide an underlying political economy of why countries might end up on good or bad equilibrium paths, beyond genuflection to the fact that they avoided the insidious effects of rent-seeking.[18] In this regard, the developmental state literature

---

[18] This failing is somewhat ironic as Krueger (1974) and Bhagwati (1982) – major proponents of the neoclassical explanation for East Asia's growth – both made

differs quite fundamentally not only from neoclassical accounts but even from those of heterodox economists primarily focused solely on the causal nexus between policy and economic outcomes. Johnson and his followers, particularly the political scientists, were not simply interested in the effects of policies but in the institutional and political arrangements that produce and implement them in the first place.

In Section 3.3, I provide an overview of three particular coordination problems: those that arise in moving from agriculture to industry and the somewhat different problems of moving into international markets and upgrading; those associated with financial markets; and issues surrounding the transfer and adoption of technology and innovation, which are particularly germane to the revival of the developmental state concept in the twenty-first century. In each case, I begin with the underlying theory and efforts to model coordination problems. I then provide examples of canonical industry cases from those writing explicitly in the developmental state and heterodox traditions, mostly from Northeast Asia but with some Southeast Asian followers included as well.

As will be seen, the timing of these examples differs somewhat depending on the country and industry in question and on what Richard Doner (2009) calls the particular "tasks" at hand. For Japan, the high developmental state period begins in the 1950s, in Korea and Taiwan from the early 1960s, and in the Southeast Asian countries from the later 1960s and 1970s. But the timeline extends into the 1980s and the move into more technology-intensive activities as well, most notably with respect to the electronics complex.

3.3 Solving Coordination Problems in the Growth Process

3.3.1 The Real Economy

Wade's dominant line of argument parallels Johnson's account of Japanese policy, as well as the thinking of a group of prominent

---

significant contributions to the literature on rent-seeking or what Bhagwati called "directly unproductive profit-seeking (DUP) activities" (Bhagwati 1982).

Japanese analysts (for example, Aoki, Kim, and Okuno-Fujiwara 1996), in focusing on coordination problems in the industrial sector. Efficient investment can be deterred by small market size and the absence of complementary suppliers or customers, as Gerschenkron (1962) had also pointed out. Rodrik (1995) outlines a basic two-sector model of such coordination problems that is tailored to the particularities of the Korea and Taiwan cases. Rodrik's model consists of a traditional sector and a capital-intensive modern sector. The modern sector yields higher returns on all factors when up and running, but relies on an array of specialized inputs, including not only capital and intermediate goods but skilled labor and technology. These inputs have several features that generate coordination problems, most notably that they exhibit increasing returns and – more controversially – they are not perfectly traded. For example, they may not conform adequately to local conditions or require specialized skills to utilize.

The model is characterized by good and bad equilibria, with high returns if and only if adequate investment is forthcoming in producing the specialized inputs. Rodrik states the coordination problem clearly:

> From the perspective of an individual investor it will not pay to invest in the modern sector unless others are doing so as well. The profitability of the modern sector depends on the simultaneous presence of the specialized inputs; but the profitability of producing these inputs in turn depends on the presence of demand from a pre-existing modern sector. It is this interdependence of production and investment decisions that creates the coordination problem. (1995, 79–80)

The implication for policy is clear: current market prices will not adequately convey information about future growth, and countries thus forego investments that would lower production costs through larger plant size and learning effects. In Amsden's (1989) infamous dictum, the East Asian countries succeeded not by "getting prices right" – as neoclassical interpretations claimed – but by "getting prices wrong." Interventions such as protection, subsidies, and rents more generally (Khan and Sundaram 2000) can overcome these collective action problems and externalities and thus push an economy from a bad to a good equilibrium. Among the more specific measures that might assist in this regard are the coordination of complementary investments across sectors, as envisioned by both Gerschenkron and theorists of the "big push"; policies to assure scale economies such as state-orchestrated mergers or financing conditional on achieving adequate scale; the coordination of potentially competing investments through entry regulation, including by foreign investors; local content and indigenization requirements; and investment cartels. For declining industries with such characteristics, the coordination problems shift to controlling investment, reducing surplus capacity, negotiating exit and sectoral as opposed to simply corporate restructuring.

Yet these purely economic arguments do not convey the institutional context required to effectively pursue such policies. As Gerschenkron noted, such problems first arise in the heavy and intermediate sectors such as steel and petrochemicals, where there are increasing returns and capital investments are large and lumpy. The challenges in these sectors center on coordinating across sectors with strong input–output linkages, reaching credible agreements and monitoring their implementation. It is thus instructive to start with a contribution by a Japanese economist, Tetsuji Okazaki (1997), in a prominent collection (Aoki, Kim, and Okuno-Fujiwara 1997) that sought to thread its way between neoclassical and developmental state interpretations.

Okazaki notes that coordination problems rapidly became evident in the 1949 meetings of the Planning Committee for Economic Reconstruction, the first general deliberative council on industrial policy in postwar Japan. Foreign exchange constraints played a critical role and exports of textiles were blocked by the closure of the Chinese and Indian markets. The findings of these early reports and complementary work carried out by the Japan Federation of Industries could not more closely mirror the Rodrik model: potential exporters of machinery, as well as the auto and shipbuilding industries, pointed to the high price of steel as a barrier to their growth. "Another aspect of interdependence," according to Okazaki, "can be seen in the fact that the production or investment level of one industry affected another industry's production level through market size, which in turn affected cost through economies of scale" (1997, 79). In the absence of coordination, linked industries would have faced a "vicious cycle" of lost competitiveness.

The outcome of these early deliberations was the formation of the Council for Industrial Rationalization as an advisory body to MITI, with no fewer than twenty-nine sectoral branches made up of industry representatives as well as bureaucrats and academic experts. Per Johnson, the objectives of these committees were not only the rationalization of production *within* each sector, but a consideration of the broader interdependence *among* them that arose through input–output linkages. Okazaki hones in on the choke point created by the relationship between the coal and steel industries: that downstream consumers of steel needed to achieve competitive prices if they were to export, but the price of steel depended on the price of coal and other upstream inputs. He details the negotiations on the prices and investments needed to permit competitiveness and the transitional subsidies and lending that would be required to meet these objectives. In these negotiations, Okazaki shows that state actors were far from passive respondents to industry demands, using policy instruments not only to corral compliance but to limit costs as well. These agreements, in turn, found their way into the investment plans of the major steel companies, supported by loans from aid counterpart funds and later by the Japan Development Bank and private lenders on the basis of information provided by MITI.

This effort clearly does not conform to the caricature of a directive state picking winners from on high. Rather, Okazaki details a complex set of negotiations, structured by both the government and the private sector within established institutions, that permitted the revelation of information around particular plans at the sector and firm level. These in turn were backed by the instruments to implement and monitor them. To be sure, these plans subsequently faced a second round of coordination problems associated with excessive investment that generated new coordination efforts to rationalize the steel sector, not all of them successful. But Okazaki's conclusions are unambiguous: in the absence of coordination, investment and output in steel would not have taken place.

Coordination problems were by no means limited to classic import-substituting industries, and as the Japanese steel case demonstrates questions of international competitiveness were evident in those discussions as well. They also arise in the initial reorientation of industrial activity toward world markets, Akamatsu's problematic. In his PhD dissertation, sociologist Thomas Gold (1980) documented how the government in Taiwan coordinated complementary investments in the textile industry during a brief phase of import-substitution in the 1950s, assuring that investments in spinning and weaving were adequate to supply the burgeoning garment sector.

Both Gold and Kuo's (1995, 95–111) detailed treatment of the industry also identifies coordination problems in the early export drive as well. The textile industry in Taiwan faced a variety of constraints at the end of the 1950s, including domestic price wars following deregulation of the industry, a strong Japanese presence in international markets, and rising protectionism abroad. From 1961, producers started to collude in a formal Contract of Cooperation that involved restraints on production, commitments to export, collective purchases and price setting of cotton, support from an industry-wide fund and even an internal arbitration committee. But this edifice of collusion was effectively state sanctioned. Kuo notes that many of the industry's requests to the government were for supporting infrastructure and a reduction of red tape that amounted to liberalization: "revisions of expansion and entry requirements, bonded factory systems, tax rebates, tariff reductions [on inputs], loan applications, administrative fees and export inspections" (107). Yet these liberalizing actions went hand in hand with a parallel set of industry requests that took a quite different form: "trade protection, restriction on foreign direct investment, low-interest loans, contract enforcement, quota negotiation and the collection of foreign market information" (107). The apparent contradiction between these two policy trends conforms with Amsden's observations about getting prices wrong. Increased market orientation during this transition phase was generally limited to the export sector, with domestic producers exempted from duties on imported inputs. But rents were generated for those venturing into export markets by protecting the domestic market, forcing consumers to subsidize producers.[19]

Among the tasks that involved coordination were unifying inspection criteria so that exported product did not face quality lapses and distributing textile quota (see also Wade 1990, 144–147). In the Korean case, the role of the state in coordinating the initial export drive in the early 1960s was even more apparent, with sectoral committees under the Ministry of Commerce and Industry linking to state-sanctioned sectoral export associations under the Korea Traders Association. These institutions set indicative targets, orchestrated incentives, and coordinated a variety of services from quality control to the collection of market information and forging linkages with buyers (Haggard, Kim, and Moon 1991). They also assured that incentives were only extended to those firms that met performance criteria, a crucial point addressed in more detail in Section 4.

Finally, it is worth noting an example of coordination in the process of upgrading and the move into altogether new technology-intensive manufacturing sectors. Gregory Noble's outstanding *Collective Action in East Asia* (1998) is of interest in this regard because it notes that such coordination does not always occur. In a deeply researched case study on the video industry, Noble identifies a clear coordination problem associated with entering a new segment: the setting of standards and even basic format. However, he shows that rather than leading, the government

[19] Similar points were made in the strategic trade policy literature that is addressed in Section 5.1.1.

lacked detailed knowledge of the industry and tended to simply support the industry mainstream. That task was complicated, however, when both independent "mavericks" and incumbents bucked the consensus. Noble argues that the epic VCR battle between Sony's Beta format and JVC's VHS ended up producing an optimal level of competition that actually strengthened the Japanese industry compared to the weakly coordinated American one. But "the struggle was hardly consistent with the rosier picture of Japanese as a neatly cooperative 'network society'" (120–121) and could not be attributed to successful coordination.

Noble's analysis of the consumer electronics industry provides a fitting conclusion to the discussion of coordination problems in the real economy. The plethora of industry studies in the developmental state literature focus not only on the initial big push in heavy industry – Gerschenkron's paradigmatic case – but in the transition to export markets and to technology-intensive activities as well.

Such studies look not only at policies, but identify the public and private institutions associated with solving specific coordination problems as well as the implementation and monitoring required for them to work. In this regard, it is important to underscore that not all work in the developmental state literature was simply "picking winners," the classic *post hoc ergo propter hoc* pitfall. Rather, studies such as Noble's show that the success of industrial policy efforts was conditional on institutional arrangements. In the Japanese steel case, MITI was at the peak of its powers, with a bevy of instruments at its disposal vis-à-vis heavy industries starved for capital. In Noble's case, the powers of the Japanese government had waned as technology outran ministerial capability to monitor and implement policy vis-à-vis a rapidly evolving industry. The private sector also exhibited greater political independence than it had in the early postwar period. In Korea, the power of the state to command was extraordinarily direct because of the authoritarian nature of the political system, the state-corporatist organization of business, and direct state control over finance. In Taiwan, by contrast, the garment industry was already strongly organized and the state role somewhat lighter. Moreover, political relationships between the Kuomintang (KMT) and Taiwanese capital were more arm's-length as we will see. Clearly, as Johnson emphasized, political as well as economic parameters were at stake in allowing industrial coordination to work.

3.3.2 The Role of the Financial Sector

A second theoretical rationale for intervention centers on failures in capital markets and provides one area where heterodox economists – including Nobel Laureate Joseph Stiglitz (Hellman, Murdock, and Stiglitz 1996) – entered the debate. Financial systems were central to Gerschenkron's analysis of nineteenth-century European industrialization and played a prominent role in accounts of postwar European industrial policy as well (for example, Zysman 1984).

Amsden (2001) notes that failures in financial markets were fairly straightforward: banking systems were wholly inadequate to the task of mobilizing the funds required for moving into basic industries and states routinely took on the role through the founding of development banks. At one point, she even goes so far as to identify development banking as one of the defining features of the developmental state, along with local content requirements, selective liberalization, and building national champions (pp. 125 ff.).

Hellman, Murdock, and Stiglitz (1996) provide a nuanced theoretical rationale for the complex regimes of "financial constraint" that typified both Japan and a number of the East Asian followers, even where banking was not in state hands. Financial restraint self-consciously seeks to create rents in the financial sector, for example by setting deposit rates below their competitive equilibrium level and by regulating entry and controlling competition. Yet rents in the financial sector – and the corresponding rents in industry from the ability to borrow on favorable terms – can have positive effects on investment. For example, such subsidies can increase equity stakes, making firms behave in a more proprietary way and induce investments that might not otherwise occur because of a divergence between social and private rates of return.

The role of the financial system in the success of the developmental states is somewhat contentious as it varies quite substantially across the three canonical cases. With respect to Japan, for example, Kent Calder's *Strategic Capitalism* (1993) purported to show that MITI was weak. Rather, the Industrial Bank of Japan (IBJ), the commercial banks, and bankers' associations were the locus of coordination on industrial policy. In explicit contrast to Johnson, Calder's analysis bears closer resemblance to Gerschenkron's account: financial institutions play the key institutional role; private interests dominate public ones; and the state's role is demoted (see Johnson 1999, 57–59 for a rejoinder; Cheng 1993 on Taiwan).

Korea, however, was a completely different story, and the central role of the financial sector in that case is the subject of Meredith Woo-Cumings' (1991) *Race to the Swift*.[20] The study takes a specifically contrarian view to neoclassical accounts by showing how the purportedly liberalizing reforms in the early 1960s – including in the financial sector – were preceded by the complete nationalization of the commercial banking sector by the Park Chung Hee junta. Woo-Cumings shows throughout her book how control over the financial sector, including foreign borrowing, allowed the government to mobilize savings and steer investment. More importantly, it also allowed the regime to exercise political control over the private sector, at least through the 1970s when the growing power of the *chaebol* yielded a more balanced relationship (for example, Kim 1997; Kang 2002). Drawing explicit parallels to Gerschenkron (1962, Woo 130), she focuses particular attention on the Heavy and Chemical Industry Plan (HCIP) of the 1970s, during which a set of six heavy industries – steel, chemical, metal, machine-building, ship-building, and electronics – were targeted not only for a round of deepening through import substitution but for entry onto global markets through exports as well.

---

[20] Taiwan presents an interesting anomaly, as the state controlled the financial system but generally used it during the high-growth phase to finance state-owned enterprises rather than private ones.

Banks were not themselves the coordinating mechanism for this effort; to the contrary, they were arguably only instruments. However Woo-Cumings and others have detailed how newly created bureaucratic structures were created by the president to direct the broader effort, "bypassing and sometimes dictating to the Economic Planning Board and the Ministry of Finance" and creating consultative mechanisms with the private sector (Woo-Cumings 1991, 129; Rhee 1994, 59–64). Nonetheless, financing mobilized through a massive National Investment Fund, preferential financing through state-owned banks, and control over foreign borrowing (while restricting FDI) were undoubtedly the key government policy tool in these efforts.

Was state financing not only effective but efficient? In one of the few studies to evaluate the success of industrial policy through a cost–benefit analysis, Stern et al. (1995, 111–112) reach mixed results. The HCIP probably changed the industrial structure of the country from what it would have otherwise been and none of the projects reviewed in detail were outright disasters. But Stern et al. claim that none exhibited evidence of truly successful industrial policy as Wade defines it: having low internal rates of return at base-year prices and a rate of return exceeding the cost of capital at current prices. We know that the planning process was followed by bouts of surplus capacity in the early 1980s that necessitated the state's stepping back in through an altogether different coordination function: reducing surplus capacity, providing financial bailouts, and reallocating investments among the major enterprises, all with obvious social costs. Rhee (1994) argues that the power to coordinate had eroded by this point, and the "too big to fail" problem severely limited the capacity of the state to rationalize heavy and chemical industry investments. Yet the success of a number of the larger *chaebol* that grew up during this era suggests that the question of the dynamic effects of state intervention through the financial sector remain open. These obvious success cases include not only private sector behemoths like Samsung but state-owned enterprises such as POSCO.

3.3.3   Technology and Learning

A third rationale for state intervention in support of industry centers on technology, the development of indigenous capabilities, and learning. Among those writing explicitly within the developmental state framework, Amsden (1989, 1991, 2001; Amsden and Chu (2003)) and Evans (1995) were most preoccupied with these issues. In recapitulating the theory of state intervention with respect to technology, intellectual lines blur because a variety of heterodox approaches to economic growth have focused on the issue.[21] Rather than review these various strands, it is best to stand aside and let Amsden speak, as she deepened thinking about what developmental states do by placing particular emphasis on learning.

In *The Rise of "the Rest"* (2001, 2), Amsden defines economic development as "a process of moving from a set of assets based on primary products, exploited by unskilled labor, to a set of assets based on knowledge, exploited by skilled labor." Explicitly following Gerschenkron and the progenitors discussed in Section 2, she places this process in an international context.

Amsden frontally attacked the neoclassical idea that latecomers can successfully borrow from first movers by focusing on comparative advantage in labor-intensive industries alone. A poor country's lower wages may still leave it uncompetitive in any given industry when coming up against a rich country's higher productivity. As a result, specialization on the basis of comparative advantage in low-technology industries – achieved through liberalization – does not necessarily work (and by implication, was not what the successful Asian latecomers actually did). The only alternative to allowing real wages to fall via a depreciating exchange rate was to subsidize learning.

---

[21] These include Nelson and Winter's (1982) *An Evolutionary Theory of Economic Change* and subsequent work on national innovation systems (Nelson 1993), the influential work of Sanjaya Lall (for example, 1996), and endogenous growth theory's efforts to explicitly incorporate technical change (Romer 1986). A distinctive feature of this new wave of endogenous growth models – and also central to heterodox ones – is the absence of diminishing returns to capital.

The justification for such measures draws on well-known imperfections in markets for technology. As Dahlman, Ross-Larson, and Pursell (1987, 762) point out, "when firms choose technology, they choose more than a method for making something at expected costs, benefits and engineering norms. They also choose the capabilities they can acquire from experience with the technology – capabilities that would enable them to move on to new activities." But developing country firms lack full information on technological alternatives, function with imperfect information on the technologies they do acquire, and are subject to variable, unpredictable, and highly path-dependent learning processes. Incomplete appropriability leads to underinvestment in research and development (R&D), foregoing the many externalities that arise around R&D activities.

Amsden's account is not one that is limited to information asymmetries, however, or constraints that might be overcome by investments in education or industry-neutral infrastructure alone. It goes to more fundamental questions of tacit knowledge and learning:

> Unlike information, which is factual, knowledge is conceptual; it involves combinations of facts that interact in intangible ways. Perfect information is conceivable – with enough time and money, a firm may learn all the extant facts pertaining to its business. Perfect knowledge is inconceivable because knowledge is firm-specific and kept proprietary as best as possible to earn technological rents. (3)

Firms play a central role in Amsden's entire corpus, and her book on Korea did not focus on the role of the state to the extent that is commonly thought. Rather, again following Gerschenkron, she was also interested in whether the internal organization of the Korean *chaebol* was conducive to the absorption and modification of technology and learning. For example, she emphasized the multidivisional structure of Korean groups, which allowed learning across related activities, and the heavy investment firms made in process engineering. Institutions mattered, but these included latecomer firms. Nonetheless, direct state investment in R&D, government requirements for licensing and technology transfer in FDI, and a variety of other subsidies to learning were crucial to building up the national champions that were the locus of innovation, productivity, and learning.

Before turning to some examples, it is worthwhile to underline that Amsden's arguments comport with more mainstream theory and empirical work on several important points. Neoclassical growth theory allowed for the possibility that countries would not only move along a given production function as capital accumulated but could shift to more productive paths, including global best practice (see Pack 2001). Such moves were linked to sectoral shifts in output, as emphasized by the postwar progenitors discussed earlier, and ultimately to the growth of larger firms using modern technology (see Amsden and Chu 2003 on Taiwan).

The contested empirical evidence from growth accounting exercises also provided at least some support for the focus on learning. To be sure, these efforts did show that factor inputs played a key role in East Asian growth, perhaps accounting for as much as two-thirds of it over the 1960–1994 period. But this is not the relevant metric. As Pack points out, total factor productivity growth in East Asia was substantially higher than in other developing countries, suggesting that something distinctive was at work in the region.[22]

We can get a sense of these processes by summarizing some exemplary case studies, this time reaching into Southeast Asian examples. In no broad sector was the question of technology and learning more central than in the rapid evolution of the Asian electronics industry, on which a vast literature emerged.[23] Singapore is a particularly interesting case to consider as it did not traverse a flying geese path from import substitution to exports. Rather, the history of the country as an entrepôt guaranteed a relatively open economy

---

[22] Among the complementary policies that might accelerate learning were the investment in education, including in higher education and engineering fields; I return to the role of social policy Section 4.

[23] Much of this literature embraced heterodox presumptions, seeing the state role as significant in the evolution of national- and firm-level capabilities in the region. See for example Hobday 1995 and Lall 1996 on regional patterns and Linsu Kim 1997 on Korea.

from the start of its industrialization drive, with foreign investment dominating the city-state's manufacturing sector.

Nonetheless, a number of accounts either cast strong doubt on market-oriented interpretations of Singapore's economic growth or placed the country squarely in the broader developmental state framework (Lim 1983; Rodan 1989; Haggard 1990;Huff 1995; Chiu, Ho, and Liu 1997; Low 1998). Compared to the governments in Japan, Korea, and Taiwan, the government in Singapore did not significantly limit FDI nor initially intervene to structure foreign firm's local operations, for example by forcing joint ventures, technology transfer agreements or local sourcing. Rather MNCs initially came to establish their own assembly operations, generating early examples of the international production networks that subsequently spanned the region.

Yet an extraordinarily capable Economic Development Board continually urged investors to upgrade by bringing in new products and introducing more advanced manufacturing processes (Schein 1997). This upgrading process was facilitated by public research institutes and training programs that effectively subsidized both capital and labor by guaranteeing a supply of highly specialized inputs and workers with sector, segment, and even firm-specific skills (Wong 1994, Wong and Ng 2001). Early stages in this process focused on process engineering capabilities through the public Singapore Institute for Standards and Industrial Research (SISIR). More specialized training institutes subsequently supported these efforts in areas where local firms were entering as suppliers to multinationals in the emerging electronics cluster.

The government was not averse to providing direct subsidies to local firms, including a Research Incentives Scheme for Companies (RISC) and a Local Industry Upgrading Scheme (LIUP). An interesting feature of LIUP is that it encouraged multinationals to provide their own staff to directly assist local suppliers in upgrading their capabilities, a textbook case of coordination. Over time – in good Akamatsu fashion – these programs evolved from upgrading process technologies to collaboration between foreign and local firms on R&D, with new public research institutes continually being devised around very particular sectoral needs. Again it is important to emphasize that these forms of coordination were not equivalent to picking winners from on high. Rather, they were more networklike: forging highly targeted capabilities by building institutions that connected the government, multinationals, and their suppliers around tasks identified by the industries themselves.

Related processes were visible in the emergence of an electronics cluster on the Malaysian island of Penang (Rasiah 1994, 1995, 2001). Rasiah's work focuses on the introduction of just-in-time production processes in the electronics sector, initially by Japanese firms. Of course, subcontracting relationships were one avenue through which these capabilities developed. But Rasiah concludes that "provision of collective goods and services" by the Penang state government and related institutions were an integral part of the process, most notably the Penang Development Corporation and the Penang Skills Development Center (PSDC). These initiatives included the formation of business councils aimed in part at "matchmaking" between foreign and local firms that reduced search costs. A well-known training effort through the PSDC cooperated with fifty-one member multinationals to provide industry-specific training to workers, the ultimate locus of learning. As Rasiah (2001, 185) concludes, "such institutional environments are most productive under public–private sector interactions through which information is widely diffused and industry-wide goods are transparently available in exchange for market-conforming performance."

3.4 A Theoretical Reprise

The developmental state literature sought to perform a difficult analytic trick: to explain particular episodes of high growth – a macroeconomic phenomenon – by invoking arguments that ultimately rested on coordination at the industry or microeconomic level. As we have seen, the methodological issues are nontrivial. There is evidence that the East Asian countries not only witnessed a rapid accumulation of capital but productivity growth that outstripped that of other developing countries. It remains an issue of debate whether case-study evidence gathered at the sectoral level is convincing for explaining aggregate economic performance. This is particularly true where the exercise appears biased toward the selection of successful cases and foregoes the complex counterfactual analysis outlined by Wade.

But much depends on where the burden of proof is assumed to lie. Neoclassical accounts attempted to show that complex policy regimes characterized by a welter of offsetting interventions in fact corresponded, in aggregate, with a structure of incentives that permitted exploitation of the country's comparative advantage. Scholars in the developmental state vein have on their side granular historical narratives that suggest a whole series of additional – if perhaps complementary – interventions. Moreover, they advance a plausible theoretical story about the pervasive role of market failures and coordination problems in the development process.

The neoclassical account also remains particularly underwhelming in its political economy. How did these policy regimes arise politically, and how did they control rent-seeking? The cases outlined here show that policy is not simply a question of turning parametric dials, and certainly does not conform with an image of a state "picking winners" from on high. Rather, the model rested on coordination and communication with private actors and complex bureaucratic capabilities in policy implementation and monitoring. Such arrangements raise important questions of political economy, to which I now turn.

4   From Policy to Politics: Institutional, Coalitional, and Historical Foundations of Developmental States

The developmental state literature frontally challenged neoclassical economic orthodoxy. Yet it also developed lines of reasoning about economic growth that ran counter to prevailing and emerging political economy models as well. The dominant institutional model of growth in economics and political science focuses on property rights and contracting, the rule of law, and checks on state power. The core theoretical point runs through two distinct but closely related channels: the effects of property rights on investment and the effects of contract enforcement on trade (Alchian 1965; Demsetz 1967; Alchian and Demsetz 1973; Besley and Ghatak 2010). These innovations were followed by applications in the new economic history, of which Douglas North was the most influential proponent (North and Thomas 1973; North 1981, 1990). They subsequently enjoyed yet another revival with observations about the significance of institutional checks on government (for example, Weingast 1995; 1997), the "rule of law" (Haggard and Tiede 2011 for a review), and the broader role of institutions in long-run growth (Acemoglu, Johnson, and Robinson 2001, 2005 Acemoglu and Robinson 2012; North, Wallis, and Weingast 2009). These more recent approaches emphasized the importance of "inclusivity" or "openness" in institutions, and particularly the importance of lowering barriers to entry in both labor and capital markets. Nonetheless, at their core they emphasized "secure property rights, the law, public services, and the freedom to contract and exchange," all of which "rely on the state, the institution with the coercive capacity to impose order, prevent theft and fraud, and enforce contracts between private parties" (Acemoglu and Robinson 2012, 79–80).

As the theoretical ideas underlying this approach have been outlined in the works cited earlier, we can treat them briefly. Property rights are social institutions that define the privileges individuals and other legal entities such as firms enjoy with respect to a given allocation of resources. These rights include those of control, the appropriation of income, and transfer. The capacity to contract is equally fundamental. Some trade can take place in the form of barter or exchanges in which transactions clear immediately. More complex transactions require the ability to make and receive promises about future actions, particularly financial transactions that from a legal point of view are basically intertemporal contracts.

Time inconsistency problems and credible commitments are crucial to understanding the significance of the rule of law.

At the private level, investments can be expropriated and contracts can be broken. Credible third-party enforcement of property rights and contract increases private returns, extends time horizons, and deters opportunistic behavior. Yet the state itself must also be checked; indeed, the predatory or "extractive" (Acemoglu and Robinson 2012) state – rather than a rent-seeking private sector – is often assumed to be the most significant challenge to growth.

It does not take much reflection to see that the East Asian growth miracles conformed only loosely, if at all, with these political desiderata. Japan was a democracy, but one in which bureaucratic discretion was high as Johnson repeatedly emphasized. Korea, Taiwan, Singapore, and Hong Kong were effectively authoritarian at the time of their growth takeoffs, as were most of the Southeast Asian followers.[24] If constitutional checks on the executive are seen as central to assuring the credibility of government policy, the paradigmatic cases did not conform to the model. Recent theoretical work has suggested ways in which the credibility problems with respect to property rights and enforcement of contracting might be solved even in the absence of formal institutional checks (Besley and Ghatak 2010). These include the well-known mechanism of reputation, but also public ownership that vests the state in rules, limited forms of voice that might nonetheless allow autocrats to send credible signals, and coherent systems of taxation that reduce incentives to outright expropriation. These new theoretical

---

[24] This experience might be given a partisan or coalitional interpretation that is consistent with a property rights story. The growth miracles in East Asia occurred during relatively long periods of political dominance by conservative parties or elites that arguably mitigated even more extreme challenges to property rights emanating from the left, as occurred in China, North Korea, Vietnam, and in more limited form in insurgencies in the Philippines and Malaysia. These right-wing governments include those under the Liberal Democratic Party (LDP), Kuomintang (KMT), and People's Action Party (PAP) in Japan, Taiwan, and Singapore, respectively; Park Chung Hee, Soeharto, and Mahathir in Korea, Indonesia, and Malaysia; the British colonial administration in Hong Kong; and a surprisingly stable alliance of king, military, and bureaucracy in Thailand.

developments open up promising avenues for revisiting the historical record, and I come back to several of them in the account that follows. Nonetheless, it is hard to escape the anomalous quality of Asia's growth when viewed through a standard property rights and contracting lens. The region was certainly not characterized by strong checks on state power, well-developed rule of law, independent judiciaries, or even well-codified property rights given the discretion exercised by strong states.

An integrated statement of the political model undergirding the developmental state is surprisingly hard to find. Nonetheless, the research tradition initially rested on two, interlinked political observations. The first, due to Johnson, centered on the state and bureaucracy. Developmental states were characterized by strong executives, but even more importantly by delegation from executives to capable and appropriately incentivized bureaucracies. Johnson's view of the Japanese polity rested on the controversial assertion – which generated its own revisionist backlash – that politicians "reigned" but that bureaucrats ultimately "ruled" through powerful highly meritocratic ministries such as MITI.

The second strand of thinking looked more closely at the relationship between the government, the private sector, and other social forces, including labor. The central claim here was that the developmental state was politically insulated, not only from the left and working class but the private sector as well.

What is the underlying theory that would justify a focus on the efficacious state as one that was centralized, internally coherent, and politically insulated? The answers trace back to the core mechanisms that generate long-run growth: on the one hand accumulation, on the other the capacity to steer investment into sectors that are dynamically efficient.

As we noted in Section 3, early growth accounting suggested that much of Asia's growth could be explained by sheer factor accumulation. This view is still contested, but any model of East Asia's growth must offer an account of the extraordinary mobilization of resources and level of investment during the high-growth period. In this regard, the developmental state literature comports with a longer-standing tradition on how the suppression of distributive demands, and even political participation, are a necessary condition in the early stages of industrialization (de Schweinitz 1964; Huntington and Nelson 1976).

However, accumulation should not yield high growth if allocated inefficiently. Even advocates of industrial policy argued for policies that were in conformity with "dynamic comparative advantage." The second political economy problem – implicit in all of the cases discussed in Section 3 – is thus one of transition. How do countries move policy from an economically and politically distorted low-growth equilibrium to a high-growth path? This second point was directly related to the theme of rent-seeking that is an undercurrent of anxiety throughout the developmental state literature and its precursors, one highlighted by both Chang (1994, 38–44) and particularly Amsden (2001).

In Amsden's felicitous phrase, a key feature of the developmental state was its capacity to "discipline" the private sector. Such discipline was the heart of what she called "control regimes" in her summary statement of the development process *The Rise of "the Rest"* (2001). The logic is worth quoting at length:

> A control mechanism is a set of institutions that imposes discipline on economic behavior. The control mechanism of "the rest" revolved around the principle of *reciprocity*. Subsidies ("intermediate assets") were allocated to make manufacturing profitable – to facilitate the flow of resources from primary product assets to knowledge-based assets – but did not become giveaways. Recipients of subsidies were subjected to *monitorable performance standards that were redistributive in nature and results-oriented*. The reciprocal control mechanism of "the rest" thus transformed the inefficiency and venality associated with government intervention into collective good, just as the "invisible hand" of the North Atlantic's market-driven control mechanism transformed the chaos and selfishness of market forces into general well-being. (8, emphasis in the original)

These observations were later extended by the World Bank (1993) and Stiglitz (1996 166) into a cognate discussion of how "contests" were used to simultaneously reward the private sector while limiting unproductive rent-seeking.

For political scientists, of course, these claims only served to push the underlying problem back one more step in the analytic chain. The question was not simply how political institutions solved rent-seeking problems, but where these institutions came from in the first place. And who guards the guardians? Why would executives with concentrated power who are effectively insulated from social forces nonetheless act in the public interest? I take up these issues in three steps. The first is to consider the role of formal institutions, most notably regime type and the bureaucracy, the classic developmental state arguments. The second is to look more closely at the social foundations of the developmental state in its relations with both capital and labor. Despite the common assumption that developmental states rested on strong pro-business alliances, this literature yielded some counterintuitive findings, including controls on the private sector and investments in human capital. The final step is a wider comparative-historical analysis of how developmental states arose in the first place, the question of origins. As will be seen, the international environment looms large in the origins literature, suggesting a variety of ways that external constraints played a role in checking strong executives.

4.1 Political Institutions, Big and Small: Regime Type and Bureaucracy

Johnson was clear that Japan's autonomous developmental state was forged under semidemocratic and authoritarian rule. Yet he was always ambivalent about whether authoritarian rule was a necessary condition for rapid growth. Japan was at least nominally democratic in the miracle years of the early postwar period, but he vehemently objected to the idea that Japan's democracy resembled the more pluralist model of the US system. Moreover, he admits in his later reflection on *MITI* (Johnson 1999, 52) that authoritarianism can "mobilize the overwhelming majority of the population to work and sacrifice for developmental projects."

As the developmental state literature migrated away from Japan to the newly industrializing countries – Korea, Taiwan, Hong Kong, and Singapore – the question of regime type was joined more directly (Cheng 1990; Haggard 1990, 254–267). I have already noted the argument that authoritarian rule might make it easier to divert resources from consumption to investment. The second route, and the one I took (Haggard 1990), focused on economic reform. Dictators can overcome collective action problems inside and outside the government that hinder the formulation of coherent policy, override both rent-seeking and populist pressures, and thus push the economy onto a more efficient growth path.[25]

I was particularly interested in underlining the irony that all of the governments that undertook reforms in the region – the darlings of the neoclassical approach – were authoritarian. Moreover, there is evidence from both Korea and Taiwan – otherwise quite different cases – that authoritarian installations were immediate precursors to political and bureaucratic realignments that facilitated the pursuit of industrial policies.

In Korea, Park Chung Hee came to power in the wake of an increasingly corrupt Syngman Rhee regime and a short period of dysfunctional democracy. Park was quite explicit in linking the 1961 coup to developmental objectives. I emphasized how the new administration cut through the complex web of rent-seeking relationships that had grown up during the period of import substitution (Haggard 1990, 54–61). To be sure, relations with labor were rapidly restructured. Unions were banned outright before being rebuilt in corporatist fashion. But early political purges specifically targeted corruption and "illicit wealth accumulation" as well, ensnaring business, bureaucratic, and even military elites. The junta arrested a number of businessmen, only freeing them

[25] These observations are not necessarily at odds with recent developments in formal political economy. See for example Besley and Ghatka (2010), drawing on earlier work by Olson (1993), about how concentrated executive authority can minimize the costs of rent-seeking.

following promises to invest in a number of new projects. Nationalization of the banking sector – again, hard to imagine in the absence of regime change – provided the new government with the tools to discipline private sector behavior. It is hard to imagine the swift turnaround in the South Korean economy absent the authoritarian turn and the fundamental restructuring of the state's relationship with the private sector.

The apparently placid technocracy that subsequently evolved in Singapore had a similarly turbulent historical origin (Haggard 1990, 103–110). Singapore's politics in the 1950s centered on an epic struggle between moderate nationalists around Lee Kuan Yew on the one hand and the left on the other, and played out both within his own People's Action Party (PAP) and the larger political arena. Lee marginalized the left by transforming the PAP into a cadre party and outmaneuvering them in the larger political arena through promises of social services, economic development, and merger with the more conservative Malaya. Exploiting a referendum on merger to gain office, the PAP government did not subsequently hesitate to invoke national security as a justification to curtail the left and bring the labor movement under corporatist control. Even the bureaucracy was subject to subtle purges and restructuring as the PAP created altogether new parastatal entities to advance their objectives. The political system drifted toward single-party dominance over the mid-1960s, setting the stage for the pursuit of an outward-oriented growth strategy centered on attracting foreign direct investment.

The finding of a link between authoritarianism and growth clearly didn't generalize, although no one in the developmental state tradition argued that it did. In 2000, Adam Przeworski and his colleagues found that controlling for income and a number of other variables, regime type had no effect on investment, the growth rate of the capital stock, or overall income growth; this finding also held when limiting the test to a sample of developing countries. But Przeworski et al. also found that the standard deviation of growth in the sample of dictatorships is much larger than in the democracies, confirming that autocracies encompass both high-growth miracles such as those found in East Asia and low-growth debacles. The failure to directly address the puzzle of why some authoritarian regimes grew rapidly while others crashed and burned was a drawback of the method of focusing on a high-growth region. But as will be seen, this shortcoming subsequently motivated the cross-regional work by Evans (1995); Kohli (2004); Doner, Ritchie, and Slater (2005), and others that sought to fill in the social context of economically successful authoritarian rule.

The second institutional feature of the developmental state – and the one that preoccupied Johnson – was the bureaucracy. It is striking how much of *MITI and the Japanese Miracle* is devoted to detailing both the position of the bureaucracy within the larger political system and MITI's internal reforms, personnel changes, and policy initiatives. Johnson was at pains to debunk the notion that politicians in Japan wielded power; indeed, he found the separation between "reigning" and "ruling," between the powers of the legislative and the executive branch, between the majority party and the mandarinate – and in the last analysis between authority and power to be the defining feature of the Japanese political system. The extended analysis of MITI's internal workings is justified by Johnson's belief that the ministry ultimately drove the policy process. The model worked because core economic responsibilities were centralized in lead or pilot agencies, such agencies were motivated by clear missions, and the bureaucracy was run on meritocratic principles with strong internal systems of both rewards (such as competitive pay and long-term career tracks) and controls (sanctions for corruption). These characteristics also served to insulate the MITI from political or private sector manipulation, in part through subtle processes of "colonizing" the Liberal Democratic Party (LDP), other ministries, and private sector organizations (Johnson 1982, 35–82, 315–324). Although the relationship between bureaucracies and growth is understudied, an innovative analysis drawing on expert evaluation by Evans and Rauch (1999) found that these observations generalized: the "Weberianness" of the bureaucracy was associated with growth in a cross-section of thirty-five middle-income developing countries.

The relationship between politicians and bureaucrats in Japan's economic decision making ended up being one of the most disputed features of Johnson's book among political scientists. Virtually from the moment the book was published, critics pointed out the role that either politicians or private sector actors played in policy formulation (Krauss and Muramatsu 1984; Samuels 1987; Okimoto 1989; Calder 1993; Noble 1998). The most blunt challenge was posed by Ramseyer and Rosenbluth (1993), who argued that Johnson's much-vaunted bureaucrats were little more than agents of the LDP.

With the benefit of hindsight, the heated debate over these issues among Japan scholars seems somewhat stilted. Johnson was hardly a culturalist and sought to outline the political and administrative rationality of the "plan rational" state. It doesn't take much work to show that asymmetric information and a host of other imperfections can upset the just-so delegation story of bureaucrats as agents advanced by Ramseyer and Rosenbluth.

However, the rational choice critique was clearly onto something important. As the developmental state model was extended to authoritarian regimes beyond Japan, it seemed particularly odd to think that bureaucrats enjoyed independence from political elites. Yet this does not rule out the possibility that authoritarian leaders saw delegation to reformed bureaucracies as crucial to their own political objectives. To be sure, pockets of bureaucratic efficiency coexisted with ministries that dispensed pork and political favors even in the Northeast Asian developmental states. Kang (2002a, 2002b) in particular emphasized that such payoffs may even have been the price for wider reforms. Nonetheless, economic reforms were typically preceded or accompanied by major bureaucratic reorganizations that concentrated economic decision-making authority in one or several lead agencies, strengthened the role of technocrats in formulating policy, reformed internal bureaucratic routines, and moved toward meritocratic recruitment. Cases showed this with respect to the Economic

Planning Board in Korea (Kim 1988; Haggard 1990; Cheng, Haggard, and Kang 1998); a succession of planning bodies in Taiwan that were created in close consultation with American aid donors and operated largely outside the existing bureaucratic structure (Haggard and Pang 1994; Cheng, Haggard, and Kang 1998; Haggard and Zheng 2013); the Economic Development Board in Singapore (Schein 1996). Even Hong Kong – with the extraordinary insulation provided by its colonial status – could be incorporated into this model (Haggard 1990, 121–124).

4.2 The Social Foundations of Developmental States

4.2.1 The Business–Government Nexus

Despite the plausibility that institutions mattered, a central critique of the developmental state approach from the outset was its relative neglect of the influence wielded by the private sector (Doner 1991; MacIntyre 1994; Evans 1995; Fields 1995; Moon and Prasad 1997; Eun Mee Kim 1997; Chan, Clark, and Lam 1998; Jayasuriya 2005).[26] All of the developmental states were led by right-wing parties or leaders, and most were authoritarian to boot. The question quickly arose of how such states overcame classic political economy risks. These included not only the disabilities arising from the lack of credible checks on executive discretion that preoccupied the property rights school, but the fact that rent-seeking was often more rather than less pronounced under authoritarian rule. How could we square a state that was strong, but not predatory, credible to the private sector, but not captured? How could strong governments send credible signals to private actors while simultaneously constraining their rent-seeking behavior? How exactly did Amsden's control regimes come into existence and work?

---

[26] Johnson is somewhat misread as excessively statist in this regard. In fact, he identified "the fundamental problem of the state-guided high-growth system" as "the relationship between the state bureaucracy and privately-owned businesses" (1982, 309).

As in the literature on the relationship between policy and economic growth and performance, there were a few interesting efforts to model these relationships formally. Grabowski (1994) and Huff, Dewit, and Oughton (2001) modeled relations between a developmental state and the private sector as a signaling game in which the government proves its credibility to the private sector by complementary investments that elicit private responses. The point was extended to the distribution of subsidies or rents in an underappreciated collection by Khan and Sundaram (2000), in which they argue that rents were crucial for eliciting dynamically efficient investments that might not otherwise have taken place at all. Kang (2002a, 2002b) showed how a "mutual hostage" relationship in Korea limited the risks of both rent-seeking and predation. Big business might have been constrained to perform by a strong state, but the size of Korean firms also allowed them to limit predation.

Motivated in part by the East Asian experience, Schleifer and Vishney (1993) provided an influential model of corruption that outlined why centralization increased efficiency even in a context of rent-seeking (see Besley and Ghatka 2010 for a generalization). In the model, rent-seekers demand a range of complementary government-supplied goods. If the state is highly decentralized, different branches of government, ministries, or bureaus pursue their own interests, pushing the cost of government-supplied goods to a suboptimal level and introducing uncertainty over property rights in those rents. Centralization did not eliminate corruption but bounded its ill effects.

In all of these models, the rents associated with industrial policy are seen not only through the lens of their *economic* effects but in terms of their *political* effects as well. Rents were seen as a signal of government intent that could overcome the disabilities of an overweening state. Similarly, political centralization in the Schleifer and Vishney model bounded the costs of corruption by solving collective action problems, pricing rents at an "appropriate" level, and in effect providing security of property rights. Interestingly, the Schleifer and Vishney approach was subsequently picked up and modified by writing broadly in the developmental state tradition, most notably Kang (2002a, 2002b) with respect to Korea and MacIntyre (2003) in his analysis the financial crisis in Southeast Asia.

How were business–government relations structured institutionally? A number of studies – following Johnson – showed that "deliberation councils" linking business and government played an important role in resolving credibility problems associated with authoritarian rule and building trust between the public and private sectors (Campos and Root 1996, Root 1996, and even World Bank 1993). Root (1996) also explains how they worked by reference to an implicit model of costly signaling:

> Tying the fortunes of many groups to the continued use of the cooperative decision-making structures raises the cost of altering the system ex post. Once councils permeate an economy, a government that unilaterally imposes its will on an industry or sector will risk undermining the value of councils for other groups, thus subverting the entire system of cooperative decision-making. Government, then, is unlikely to abide only by those decisions it prefers, overturning those it opposes … By institutionalizing deliberative councils, government reduces its discretionary power but gains the confidence of business in the stability of agreed upon policies. (12)

Evans (1995), Maxfield and Schneider (1997), Weiss (1998), and Moon and Prasad (1997) all cast the argument in more general terms, claiming that a complex of both formal and informal networks between the public and private sectors played a central political role in East Asia's growth: by providing information to bureaucrats and facilitating solutions to the collective action problems identified in Section 3.3.

The existence and operation of business councils is thoroughly documented for Japan by Johnson (1982), Okimoto (1989), and others writing in the developmental state vein. The early Korean experience of export-promotion meetings chaired personally by Park Chung Hee is also a frequently used example (Haggard, Kim, and Moon 1991). Yet as we move beyond these two Northeast Asian cases, the evidence thins, and there are questions about Taiwan as well. Wade argued that Taiwan had a "corporatist" political system. However this designation didn't fit standard political science usage as Taiwanese business was certainly not organized in centralized peak associations. The Southeast Asia cases also experienced rapid growth but did not appear to have similar levels or types of state intervention as their Northeast Asian counterparts nor the institutions of coordination (MacIntyre 1994; Jomo et al. 1997).

Moreover, empirical studies of the region raised serious doubts about the capacity of Southeast Asian states to "discipline" their private sector constituents. In Malaysia, consultative institutions at the federal level did not appear until 1991, when Mahathir's "Look East" campaign sought to emulate the Northeast Asian NICs. Yet in a succession of outstanding studies, Gomez (1991; Gomez and Jomo 1997) detailed how this period was the high point of corruption, cronyism, and the interpenetration of government, state, and party. In his 1994 collection on business–government relations in Asia, MacIntyre (1994) stated the claim more generally: the Southeast Asian countries simply did not fit the macro models of business–government relations derived from the Northeast Asian cases.

These debates go to the very heart of what we mean by the developmental state. The original literature sought to characterize whole countries, drawing on an ideal type that included both economic policies and institutions for coordination as well as broader political structures, such as strong states and Weberian bureaucracies. But as the developmental state literature migrated to Southeast Asian and beyond, the findings were read to suggest more discrete ways in which states and private sectors might cooperate to solve collective action problems in the growth process. In effect, you could have intermediate types, or more accurately parts of the state – in the form of particular bureaucracies or subnational jurisdictions – that conformed to the model even if the larger political setting did not.

This approach was explicit or implicit in a second generation of industry studies that drilled down into local and sector-specific political relationships between public and private actors. In the developmental state tradition, Peter Evans' (1995) *Embedded Autonomy: States and Industrial Transformation* was particularly important in this regard. Evans begins with a stylized distinction between predatory states such as Zaire – in which purely persona-listic relations dominate and the bureaucracy is weak – and devel-opmental states that are efficacious, with Korea as the model. Brazil and India constituted "intermediate" cases in which examples of successful intervention could be found even if the broader state apparatus did not approximate the developmental state model.

The apparent oxymoron of a state that is both embedded and autonomous refers to the simultaneous existence of rationalized bureaucratic institutions *à la* Johnson that limit rent-seeking *and* dense network ties with the private sector that provided informa-tion and made for coherent policy formulation and implementa-tion. Evans appears to appropriate Johnson's *MITI*, but at the same time subtly sides with his critics such as Okimoto (1989) by empha-sizing the bureaucracy's network connections. In one of the more general statements, he writes:

> Either side of the combination by itself would not work. A state that was only autonomous would lack both sources of intelligence and the ability to rely on decentralized private implementation. Dense connecting networks without a robust internal structure would leave the state incapable of resolving "collective action" problems, of transcending the individual interests of its private counterparts. Only when embeddedness and autonomy are joined together can a state be called developmental. (Evans 1995, 12)

Evans sought to demonstrate these relationships not at the national level but by focusing on the information technology indus-try. Evans admits that at the outset the Korean model was more top-down and directive than the Japanese one. But in a process he calls "husbandry," an entrepreneurial state bureaucracy worked with leading *chaebol* groups to achieve Wade's counterfactual: to "push the local information technology sector forward just a bit faster than it would have gone on its own" (1995, 141). Among the instruments for doing so was a succession of highly focused upgrading projects that resemble the technology cases described in the previous section. For example, the 4-Megabit DRAM Project operated through an Electronics and Telecommunications Research Institute (ETRI) with more than a thousand researchers and a $120 million budget. The political point is that these were not efforts led by the state in isolation; rather, they incorporated the *chaebol* in the planning and implementation process from the outset, down to collaboration between government and private sector researchers. As Evans concludes, "ETRI's job was not to do the research and development, its task was to stimulate and coordinate efforts by the major chaebol to develop the chips themselves" (141). Evans even distinguishes the more- and less-successful Korean and Indian cases precisely by the extent to which the state was networked. Portions of the Indian bureaucracy got the "state" right, but were hampered by the lack of effective ties with private firms.

Despite this effort at comparison, Evans' work suffers from the general *post hoc ergo propter hoc* problem that critics of the developmental state literature have harped on. Selecting on the dependent variable – a successful IT initiative – he shows that it involved state programs and sector-specific institutions that were rooted in close government-business relations. Much harder is to select on the *independent* variable: to formulate a clear *ex ante* picture of the political coalitions that govern the state or any given sector and use that characterization to generate expectations about policy and economic outcomes.

Unfortunately, surprising few studies undertake this more challenging approach. Particularly nuanced examples of this type of work can be found in Noble's (1998) *Collective Action in East Asia* discussed in Section 3, David Kang's (2002a) revisionist account of Korea's developmental state in *Crony Capitalism: Corruption and Development in Korea and the Philippines,* and Richard Doner's (2009) *The Politics of Uneven Development: Thailand's Growth in Comparative Perspective.* Doner's study tracks the sugar, textile, and auto sectors over time; Table 1 offers my interpretation of the causal logic and empirical approach of the book by considering his auto industry case study.

Table 1 Doner's Analysis of the Thai Auto Industry

Period	Political Configuration	Industry Challenge	Outcome
1958–1973	Authoritarian rule, but with state divided between technocratic and clientelistic ministries and agencies	First stage of industrialization (1961–1977)	Successful in inducing entry, including through local content requirements. Initially successful government–business cooperation to assure efficiency but less successful over time in ability to rationalize the industry
1973–1979	Democratization and greater ministerial clientelism in context of highly fragmented party system		
1979–1988	Consolidation of party system and balance between technocratic and business interests	Deepening localization and first phases of export-oriented growth (1978–1988)	Success at deepening localization and driving toward scale economies and particular products, with support of government–business networks; technocratic discipline of business; but inattention to other elements of competitiveness

| 1988–1997 | Party factionalization and increase in pork | Liberalization and internationalization (1988–1997) | Success at internationalization in part from residual technocratic influence, in part because congruent with MNC strategies; less success in policies finessing losers, technical information, and coordination because of lack of industry expertise in government and fragmentation of industry associations; indigenous capabilities and backward linkages lag |

Doner's political analysis of Thailand's "intermediate state" – following Evans – begins by distinguishing phases of Thai politics based on the balance between technocratic and rent-seeking influences over time.[27] He identifies this balance as characteristic of the "coalition" in power. He then maps these coalitional configurations onto particular challenges or upgrading "tasks" the industries under consideration faced at any given point in time. The parallels to the developmental state tradition are clear: when bureaucracies are coherent and have at least somewhat greater industry-related expertise, the industry not only upgrades but local capabilities deepen. When the bureaucracy is pulled toward pork-barrel politics and the industry is fragmented, the development of local capabilities lags.

Doner's study shows how hard it is to hit the sweet spot that aligns bureaucratic autonomy and competence with private sector organization. And his study is also a reminder that these relationships can be forged at the local or sectoral as well as national level. Yet the deeper point should not be lost. The developmental state literature makes clear that simply talking about policy in the absence of institutions and underlying political alignments is unlikely to generate compelling explanations of – or prescriptions for – long-run growth.

4.2.2   Labor Subordination and the Productivist Welfare State

Just as the developmental state is associated with close business–government alliances, so it has been identified with labor subordination. As already seen, one theoretical justification for the significance of authoritarian rule was precisely to control distributive pressures emanating from the left and labor. Yet a focus on control alone does not capture the fact that the developmental states were associated with a distinctive welfare regime as well. A core feature of that regime was precocious investment in

---

[27] The discussion here omits the post-financial crisis period, which is taken up in more detail in Section 5.

education, widely seen in both orthodox and developmental state accounts as an important determinant of the region's long-run growth and of its relatively equitable income distribution.[28]

Prior to and following Johnson, a number of works had noted the relatively weak role that labor occupied in the Japanese political system, and the link between labor weakness and the broader functioning of the country's political economy (for example, Pempel and Tsunekawa 1979; Garon 1987). The most overarching comparative statement of the claim linking the industrialization of subsequent followers to labor control is Frederick Deyo's (1989) *Beneath the Miracle: Labor Subordination in the New Asian Industrialism* (see also Deyo 1981 on Singapore). The central claim of Deyo's book is simple. Given the importance of competitive wages to the export-oriented approach favored by the neoclassical account, the East Asian cases enjoyed particular advantages from the exclusion of labor.[29] These advantages were both macroeconomic and microeconomic. Developmental states were not able to fully manage the path of wage growth. After the absorption of surplus labor from agriculture, the industrial sector saw steadily rising real wages, and Campos and Root (1996) went so far as to characterize the East Asian experience as a "shared growth" model. But labor control probably dampened real wage growth, a constant concern of business in a region characterized by the recurrent entry of lower-wage "flying geese."

---

[28] I set aside here the important question of the countryside, and particularly the way land reforms might have facilitated the subsequent growth trajectory of the developmental states. On these issues, see the comparative work of Jong-sung You (2015).

[29] In her well-known methodological manifesto, Barbara Geddes (2003) challenges the claim that the weakness of labor facilitated export-led growth strategies by showing that the more general relationship between labor weakness and economic growth does not hold. According to Geddes, the developmental state literature was guilty of selection bias: drawing faulty inferences from cases selected once again on the dependent variable. But as we have noted throughout, scholars working on the developmental state – and in the deeper lineage of which it is a part – typically had relatively modest presumptions about the ability to generate general lawlike statements. The question is not whether labor weakness facilitated growth on average but whether it had a contributory effect in a quite particular institutional and historical context.

The weakness of the left and labor limited distributive pressures on taxes and spending, and particularly welfare spending. At the shop floor level, labor control increased managerial flexibility and permitted highly paternalistic industrial relations at the firm level.

Deyo does not argue that labor relations were necessarily reforged in the wake of transitions to export-led growth, but I provided some evidence in this regard (Haggard 1990) and Im (1987) makes the case for a link between industrial deepening and bureaucratic-authoritarianism in Korea. Deyo does show, however, that the greater the capacity of workers to organize – for historical or organizational reasons – the more actively the state was likely to intervene to force industrial relations into a state-corporatist mode. He contrasts Hong Kong and Taiwan, with their relatively weak union histories and the more contentious labor politics of Singapore and Korea.

These contradictory tendencies – labor control coupled with rising real incomes, improvement in other physical quality-of-life measures, and relatively equal income distribution – raise the question of whether the developmental state was associated with a particular social policy regime (for example, Goodman and Peng 1996; Goodman, White and Kwon 1997; Kwon 1997; Ramesh and Asher 2000; Ramesh 2004; Holliday 2000; Gough 2001; Holliday and Wilding 2003; Haggard and Kaufman 2008). The short answer was "yes." On the one hand, the developmental states of East Asia took a relatively minimalist approach to the provision of social insurance, whether measured by the extent of public commitment, the nature of financing, or the breadth and depth of coverage.

At the same time, governments invested early in the development of human capital (for example, Birdsall, Ross, and Sabot 1995; Ranis, Stewart and Ramirez 2000). The extent of government commitment to provision of basic health care remains an issue of debate and there are variations on this score across the region.[30]

---

[30] McGuire (2001, 2010) for example argues that the improvement in health outcomes in a number of East Asian countries owed as much to rapid income growth as to the extent and quality of public provision.

But particularly in Korea, Taiwan, Singapore, and Malaysia, governments provided early and strong support for the expansion of primary education and, with the important exception of Thailand, a timely shift to support the expansion of secondary and tertiary education as well.[31]

The combination of labor controls and investment in human capital raises broader issues about the political foundations of the developmental state. The existence of productivist welfare regimes suggests – *à la* the varieties of capitalism approach – that the region's industrial policies were nested in a much wider institutional configuration in which industrial and social policies were complementary. As will be seen in Section 5, the question of ongoing support for the development of human capabilities became a central theme in reshaping Asia's developmental states as they became more economically open and democratic and is a theme in the current revival of the developmental state concept.

4.3 Origins: The Historical Foundations of Developmental States

To sum up the discussion of politics so far, the developmental state literature innovated not only with respect to policy but in thinking about the role of political institutions and the social foundations of growth. In contrast to models that emphasized checks on state power, the rule of law, and property rights, the developmental state model emphasized strong or "insulated" states, coherent bureaucracies with ample capacity, and particular state–society relationships. Institutionalized business–government relations supported private sectors, including through the distribution of rents. But at the same time, these arrangements limited the scope of rent-seeking and made government support conditional on private sector performance. Labor regimes – while varied – limited

---

[31] This observed pattern in these regional studies was subsequently confirmed in cross-regional work on middle-income welfare states (Haggard and Kaufman 2008; Rudra 2008).

distributive pressures on the state and expanded managerial autonomy while also investing in human capital.

As Johnson argued with respect to Japan, these political arrangements did not simply emerge in response to the challenges of development; if they did, the whole world would be rich. Was it possible that the taproot of growth did not lie in institutions or proximate political configurations but in longer-run features of state–society relations? These questions produced a closer examination of the origins of developmental states, and with an important methodological turn as well. Much of the pioneering work on the developmental state took the form of country case studies. The small-n, cross-regional comparisons that characterized the "origins" literature, by contrast, sought to increase explanatory leverage by comparing the high-growth East Asian cases to countries that had more mixed records or that had failed to grow over long periods of time (Evans 1995; Waldner 1999; Kang 2002a; Chibber 2003; Kohli 2004; Doner, Slater, and Ritchie 2005; Vu 2010; Centeno, Kohli, and Yashar 2017). Such comparisons were seen as central to causal inference and thus provide an interesting juxtaposition to work on the institutional sources of long-run growth in economics that had a similar methodological objective (for example, Acemoglu and Robinson 2012).

What might account for the emergence of developmental states over the long run? A striking feature of the origins literature was a focus on the international context in which developmental states emerged. Colonialism was a natural place to start. Cumings (1984) had noted the Japanese colonial origins of the developmental states in Taiwan and Korea. Atul Kohli's (2004) *State-Directed Development: Political Power and Industrialization in the Global Periphery* generalized the argument and was one of the first to tie the literature on the developmental state into the wider debate on state formation. State structures, Kohli argued, were the product of unusual concentrations of power and coercive capability. They did not suddenly appear in response to the functional demands of some development strategy; rather, the causal arrows ran the other way. Once put in place, "core institutional characteristics acquired during colonial rule have also proved difficult to alter. Anticolonial nationalist movements were one potential organized force capable of altering the basic state forms inherited from colonialism," but for the most part such movements in Asia and Africa "were too superficial and/or fragmented to alter the inherited state forms decisively" (Kohli 2004, 17). Subsequent state forms – what Kohli called cohesive-capitalist states, fragmented-multiclass states, and neopatrimonial states – were thus the products of different types of colonial rule and the social coalitions that underpinned them.

In Korea and Taiwan, Kohli argued, the developmental state could be traced to Japanese colonial policies of building coherent bureaucracies, strong ties to private actors, and a massive repressive apparatus for dealing with class challenges from below. Despite the tumult of the 1950s, particularly the war on the Korean peninsula, these institutions survived to a surprising degree. At the other extreme, Nigeria was ruled by the British "on the cheap." Indirect rule resulted in the persistence of personalist and patrimonial relations and weak states that failed to develop even the basic capacity to extract taxes. Kohli's analysis thus provides an interesting counterpoint to Acemoglu, Johnson, and Robinson's (2001) widely cited work on the adverse effects of predatory states. Kohli argued that European colonialism in Africa had adverse long-run effects on growth, not because it predated on native populations and failed to protect property rights but because it never developed adequate state capacity or the bureaucratic institutions required for development.[32]

Kohli's story raised classic questions of the nature of historical explanation. How, for example, do we square the disadvantages

---

[32] As with Evans, Kohli notes intermediate cases, including India and Brazil. The Indian nationalist movement altered British colonial structures to a certain extent. The Estado Novo (1937-1945) and period of military rule (1964-1984) reflected periods of state "hardening" in Brazil. But Kohli stresses the persistence of inherited political and social structures. In Brazil, for example, the power of landed oligarchs, local authoritarianism, and a weak central government lingered for at least a century after decolonization and traces of these historical residues can be found to this day.

that Brazil appeared to inherit with its very high growth in the half-century prior to the debt crisis and growth collapse of the 1980s? And how do we square the developmental state institutions implanted by Japan during the colonial period in Korea with the weak performance of the Korean economy in the first post-colonial decade? Even if we take into consideration the costs of war, the Japanese inheritance certainly seemed squandered under Rhee before the turnaround under Park Chung Hee in the early 1960s (Haggard, Kang, and Moon 1997). Were we searching too far back in history to locate sources of economic performance that appeared to be more proximate?

Not all of the literature went back to colonial origins. The security setting was also a focus, and one that could encompass both Japan and later followers. Bellicist theories of state formation in Europe had long noted the close relationship between security threats and state formation (Tilly 1985). As Johnson notes, the origins of the developmental state in Japan could ultimately be traced back to the Meiji restoration, when government and business were faced with imperial encroachments in the region and the risk of unequal treaties that would consign Japan to a semicolonial status similar to China's. External threats focused the attention of both government officials and the private sector on political as well as economic catch-up and even achieving great power status.

The onset of the Cold War in East Asia and the proximity of external security threats contributed to the "hardening" of the state in both Korea and Taiwan and created strong incentives for growth-oriented policies there as well (Woo-Cumings 1991; Kang 2002). Alliance relationships with the United States created incentives on both sides of the Pacific to deepen economic ties, and the US extended massive aid to Japan, Korea, and Taiwan in the early postwar period. The US also tolerated free-riding on the part of Asian allies pursuing surprisingly inward-looking and closed economic strategies. But external security challenges also helped explain why strong states had limited scope for predatory behavior. As Herbst (1990) argued with respect to Africa in an intriguing counterfactual, it was the absence of external security threats that permitted the development of patrimonial regimes.

The external environment also played a role in models grounded ultimately in resource endowments. Since the literature by economists on the East Asian experience drew a comparison between import-substituting and export-oriented growth paths, the comparison between the East Asian cases and the middle-income countries of Latin America was a natural focus (Evans 1989, 1995; Haggard 1990; Gereffi and Wyman 1990). Why did import substitution persist and "deepen" in Latin America while the East Asian countries could shift course toward greater reliance on exports?[33] Was this outcome simply the result of contemporaneous institutions and political alignments, or were deeper constraints at work?

I focused on how external shocks interacted with underlying resource endowments to generate divergent trajectories between East Asia and Latin America (Haggard 1990). In the face of external shocks, larger developing countries such as Argentina, Brazil, and Mexico – and particularly those endowed with natural resources – could continue financing ISI despite the constraints it placed on manufactured exports. These countries were more likely to move into secondary import substitution ("deepening") than smaller countries that lacked natural resources and did not have similar domestic-market opportunities. When hit with external shocks, these smaller, resource-poor economies were more likely to adjust by following the Akematsu flying geese model of export-oriented industrialization. I noted that the shocks of interest in Korea and Taiwan included a precipitous decline in aid from the United States, which triggered a scramble for new sources of foreign exchange in exports, foreign investment, and borrowing.[34]

---

[33] This comparative work had the advantage of being able to draw on debates in Latin America about similar processes, particularly O'Donnel's (1973) model of bureaucratic authoritarianism (BA), which bore a clear family resemblance to developmental state ideas. Compare for example Kaufman 1979 on Latin America and Im 1987 on BA in Korea.

[34] I also noted that reforms that appeared to be market conforming – trade, exchange rate, and financial market reforms – were in fact designed to maximize

In one of the more important contributions to the origins literature, Doner, Slater, and Ritchie (2005) gave the argument about
external constraints an institutional twist. They argued that foreign
exchange and revenue constraints – including those associated
with the absence of natural resources – were crucial determinants
of efficiency-enhancing reforms of state structures themselves.

Although international factors emerge strongly in the origins
literature, a central issue was also the longer-run interplay between
the state and social forces: characteristics of politics that predated
the emergence of developmental states. Most significant in this
regard were inclusion or exclusion of business and labor and the
path dependencies that result. Chibber (2003, 2014) shows how
Indian business played a crucial political role in limiting the autonomy of planning agencies. Wedded to "subsidies as gifts," they had
no interest in the "discipline" – or "subsidies as contracts" – that
planners wanted to wield over investment decisions. Business interests were wedded to protection in both East Asia and Latin America
as well, but the sheer duration of import substitution in Latin
America entrenched the strategy more deeply. It would have
required a particularly powerful and independent state to shift
policy in a more outward-oriented direction in the Latin American
cases. Not surprisingly, it is only in Chile under Pinochet that we see
a transition to a more outward-oriented strategy that bears a family
resemblance to the East Asian cases, even if based on quite different
sources of comparative advantage.

In Latin America, labor incorporation was also an aspect of the
state-building process in a number of the larger economies,
including Mexico, Brazil, and Argentina, despite subsequent periods of authoritarian labor exclusion. Long periods of import substitution not only entrenched protectionism, but complex systems
of unequal social entitlements that were ultimately rooted in
employment in import-substituting activities (Haggard and
Kaufman 2008). Labor was never a core political partner in any of

political leaders' control of resources; see the discussion of Woo-Cumings
(Woo 1991) in Section 3.

the Asian newly industrializing countries. Where labor had been active, it was quickly restrained in the anticommunist authoritarian regimes that were on the frontline of the Cold War, particularly Korea and Taiwan.

Over time, the "origins" literature widened from the East Asia–Latin America comparison to encompass the Middle East, South Asia, and Africa, yet with quite similar themes of how state formation was related to different configurations of underlying social forces. Waldner (1999) argued that a key difference between Turkey and Syria on the one hand and Korea and Taiwan on the other was the breadth of the coalitions elites forged at the time that states were being formed. In Syria and Turkey, "premature" pressures to widen social coalitions gave rise to what Waldner called "precocious Keynesianism": states that were committed to growth-inhibiting transfers. Kohli (2004) similarly noted that "fragmented multi-class states" – represented in his four-country comparison by Brazil and India – precluded pro-business policies. Evans described Brazil as an "intermediate" case – between developmental and predatory states – in which clientelistic links to business and labor eroded the capacity to orchestrate a successful entry into global IT markets.

By contrast, all four of these cross-regional comparisons emphasized the presence of the features outlined earlier in the East Asian cases: relatively autonomous states and coherent bureaucracies that were able to limit transfers (Waldner), develop a distinctively pro-business environment (Kohli), or coordinate with the private sector in order to advance international competitiveness (Evans).

The findings of the work on the origins of developmental and other states raised one of the most vexing problems for comparative historical analysis. The focus on the East Asian cases was driven by pressing pragmatic concerns; an interest in the sources of rapid growth in obvious success cases. What were we to make of arguments – also visible in the economics literature (Acemoglu, Johnson, and Robinson 2001) – that the success of these cases was rooted in the colonial era or particular international contexts? Was history fate? Or could meaningful policy lessons still be extracted for national settings in which these long-term "prerequisites" were absent? These and other issues arose as developmental states were themselves transformed and the international environment changed.

5 The Fall and Rise of the Developmental State

The developmental state literature took off in the 1980s and 1990s, but it was largely preoccupied with a much earlier period. Although published in 1982, Johnson's book built up to the great industrial transformation in Japan in the 1950s and 1960s. The subsequent literature on the newly industrializing countries of Asia looked back to core "takeoff" periods: the 1960s and 1970s in Korea, Taiwan, Hong Kong, and Singapore, extending into the 1980s in Southeast Asia, at least in particular regions and industries. The origins literature, by definition, reached back still further in time. However, economic and political changes in the 1980s and 1990s raised the question of whether the developmental state model still pertained or was relevant elsewhere. As the leading exemplars of the developmental state model gradually liberalized their economies and some became democratic, the concept increasingly appeared a largely historical construct: an explanation for an unusual period of very high growth limited to a surprisingly small group of Asian success stories.

In fact, reports of the death of the developmental state were premature. Advocates of industrial policy had long argued that its advantages did not require fully replicating the development path of the East Asian cases, in any case an impossible task. Other latecomers might still learn from their experiences to develop sectoral or geographically localized interventions and institutions. By the end of the 2000s, ideological winds had shifted against the market triumphalism of the Washington consensus and early post–Cold War period, increasing receptivity to these messages even among mainstream economists (for example, the so-called Spence Report [Commission on Growth and Development 2008).

The global financial crisis of 2008 was an important turning point in this regard. The crisis called into question Anglo-Saxon models, focused attention on China's continuing success with an authoritarian-statist developmental path, and set in train a quest for a "post-Washington consensus" (Birdsall and Fukuyama 2011).

In the early twenty-first century, the developmental state concept saw a revival. Two regional examples suggest how the geographic scope of the debate widened. Within Asia, it was only a matter of time before efforts were made to identify a distinctive Chinese model (Ramo 2004, Kennedy 2010, Zhao 2017 for a review). Not surprisingly, a number of analysts sought to locate the Chinese experience within the broader developmental state tradition (for example, Baek 2005; Knight 2012). There is some question whether it is possible to assimilate the Chinese case into *any* replicable model. Given its unusual size and political and growth trajectory, it is far from clear if there are any lessons that other countries can learn from the Chinese experience (Naughton 2010). But at least superficially, some elements appeared to fit: high growth driven by an authoritarian regime, a reasonably competent and incentivized bureaucracy, a strong emphasis on fixed capital investment, and selective liberalization coupled with targeted industrial policies.

Moreover, even where the debate about China's growth path was not specifically linked to the developmental state literature, it was hard to avoid the parallels. No less than the (Chinese) chief economist of the World Bank defended the value of industrial policy for China and advanced a broader model of growth for middle- and low-income countries in which the state would "facilitate structural change by aiming to provide information, compensate for externalities, and co-ordinate improvements in the 'hard' and 'soft' infrastructure that are needed for the private sector to grow in a manner consistent with the dynamic change in the economy's comparative advantage" (Lin and Monga 2011 265; Lin 2009). The significance of these claims can be gauged from the drama surrounding the epic controversy that Lin's claims sparked with other Chinese academics such as Zhang Weiying, who argued for a more liberal course. Familiar debates were once again being replayed.[35]

The resurgence of interest in the developmental state was by no means limited to China's success. Africa became a somewhat surprising theater for the debate as well (Mkandawire 2001, 2017; Edigheji 2005, 2010; Meyns and Musamba 2010; Routley 2014). In a scathing indictment, Thandika Mkandawire (2001) challenged "the impossibility theorem": the idea that African states were too dependent, weak, incompetent, and corrupt to emulate the East Asian developmental states. Political scientists working on the region had long focused on the patrimonial nature of African governments, and some of the comparative historical work cited earlier – including both Evans (1995) and Kohli (2004) – had explicitly identified African examples as paradigms of nondevelopmental states. Mkandawire argued, however, that "most of the analyses about African states that have led to so much despondency about the prospects of development are based on invidious comparison between African states in crisis and idealized and tendentiously characterized states elsewhere" (Mkandawire 2001, 290). Rather than seeking to finesse Africa's governance problems through weakening the state and focusing on liberalization, policy should aim to strengthen state capacity (Fritz and Menocal 2006) and "get interventions right."

Nor was the literature limited to regional examples; a wide array of contributions sought to revive the concept of the developmental state more broadly (Robinson and White 1998; Sandbrook et al. 2007; Evans 2011; Evans and Heller 2015; Paus 2012; Williams 2014; Centeno, Kohli, and Yashar 2017). In looking at the resurgence of interest in the developmental state and industrial policy more generally, I first consider how the international economic landscape has changed and the constraints this placed on old models,

---

[35] See "Plan vs. Market: China's Industrial Policy," *The Economist,* November 5, 2016, at www.economist.com/news/finance-and-economics/21709561-plan-v-market.

particularly in the need for what might be called "open economy industrial policies."

Following the logic of Sections 3 and 4, I turn first to the economic policy issues and the debate that has arisen over industrial policy as a response to the so-called middle-income trap. Once again, institutions of coordination continue to play a central role in discussions of effective economic policy making, including at the sectoral level. I then turn to the politics, starting with a resurgence of interest in the concept of state capacity that again calls into question the property rights and "rule-of-law" models of growth. Yet the question of the social underpinnings of new development models remains the most pregnant and complex. What are the political coalitions that might support new developmental state models in a more democratic context? What would a "democratic developmental state" look like?

5.1 Developmental States in Their International Context: Trade Politics, Crisis, and Open Economy Industrial Policy

In Section 4 I alluded briefly to the auspicious timing of East Asia's export drive. Developmental states achieved their growth peaks just as the United States was leading a major multilateral liberalization effort through the GATT. Yet three international developments constrained both the original developmental states and limited the ability of followers to fully emulate their strategies. First, the US and Europe became less and less accepting of the "free-riding" of Japan and the Asian newly industrializing countries, pushing them to liberalize. Second, dominant interpretations of the Asian financial crisis of 1997–1998 attributed it to misguided state intervention and generated strong pressures from the US and multilateral institutions for market-oriented reforms as well. Finally, although foreign direct investment had been a crucial aspect of East Asia's development from the start, international production networks deepened significantly from the 1980s. This development fundamentally changed incentives with respect to the foreign sector. The idea that countries could succeed by promoting national champions through restrictions on trade and investment became increasingly anachronistic. A quest for a new set of policy tools – "open economy industrial policy" –sought to ensure that the benefits of integration into such networks would be maximized.

5.1.1 The International Political Economy of the Developmental States: Trade Politics

While the neoclassical revival heralded export-oriented policies as a recipe for other developing countries to follow, their very success generated a quite different conversation in the advanced industrial states. William Cline (1982) asked the simple question of whether the East Asian model of development rested on a fallacy of composition. If all developing countries pursued it, their combined manufactured exports would eventually trigger protection in industrial countries. Concerns about "deindustrialization" had already surfaced among heterodox economists in Great Britain in the 1970s (for example Kaldor 1971; Singh 1977) and trade was by no means the only factor implicated. But it did not take long for the role of Japan and the newly industrializing countries to become front and center in debates about industrial decline in the US and Europe (for example, Bluestone and Harrison 1982; Singh 1989; Wood 1994). These debates have continued unabated ever since (for example, Autor, Dorn, and Hanson 2013) and gained new salience with the emergence of nationalist and protectionist political movements in the United States and Europe.

In fact, Cline's prediction of a Northern policy response had already come to pass well before his cautionary article appeared. In the early 1980s, a number of studies approached the rise of the newly industrializing countries from the other side of the Pacific. The "new protectionism" in the US was a direct response to the rise of the newly industrializing countries of East Asia and Latin America, with a history that extended all the way back to early voluntary export restraints on cotton textiles with Japan in the late 1950s (Zysman and Tyson 1983; Yoffie 1983; Aggarwal 1983.

As comparative advantage continually shifted, in line with flying geese expectations, protection similarly moved from labor-intensive manufactures such as textiles and footwear, to consumer electronics, steel, autos, and ultimately into more technology-intensive products such as semiconductors (for example, Tyson 1993).

A crucial justification of the new protectionism was that competitive pressures arose from government actions and strategic behavior on the part of firms operating in oligopolistic markets: subsidies, exchange rate manipulation, dumping, government lending at preferential interest rates, tax benefits, and outright government ownership of firms. In short, the new protectionism was precisely targeting the policies that advocates of the developmental state had identified as sources of East Asia's success. A burgeoning literature on strategic trade policy – implicitly concerned with countering the behavior of the East Asian developmental states and state-owned European entities – had the ironic effect of providing a theoretical rationale for exactly the type of interventions pursued by these governments (see Krugman 1986 and Brander 1995 for reviews). In an early contribution to the debate, for example, Krugman (1984) showed how import protection could act as a form of export promotion in industries subject to increasing returns, learning-by-doing, and other dynamic economies. He then went on with Baldwin (Baldwin and Krugman 1988) to actually calibrate the model to markets for random access memory (RAM) computer chips. One finding of particular interest was that while Japan appears to have experienced net losses from protection in the form of higher prices, simulations suggested that free trade policies would have prevented the chip industry from even emerging in the first place!

These trade policy debates not only generated protection, they also put pressure on the newly industrializing countries to liberalize their own economies. In this regard, the term "new protectionism" is subtly misleading, since it not only reflected what might be called "import politics" but a preoccupation with "export politics": expanding opportunities for US exporters and investors abroad. The new trade policy agenda pursued through the Uruguay Round negotiations as well as what Bhagwati and Patrick (1991) called "aggressive unilateralism" placed pressure on the very instruments that had contributed to developmental state success. The irony did not go unnoticed by proponents of the developmental state model, including both Amsden (2001, ch. 9) and Chang (2002). Both saw ideological dynamics on the part of first movers quite similar to those pointed out by Alexander Hamilton more than two centuries before. The important point for our purposes is that Japan, Korea, and Taiwan were pressed to make market-opening moves, and the second-generation of Southeast Asian and other newly industrializing countries all operated in a trade policy environment that was much less tolerant of the industrial policies of the past.

5.1.2 Interpreting the Asian Financial Crisis: Moral Hazard and Cronyism

Japanese growth slowed down dramatically in the early 1990s, and the Asian financial crisis of 1997–1998 brought growth in a number of the high-performing Asian economies – most notably Thailand, Malaysia, Indonesia, and Korea – to a screeching halt. These events immediately generated a debate about the relationship among industrial policy, moral hazard, and economic vulnerability. As we have seen, governments used the financial sector – whether public or private – to induce investments in targeted activities. Yet these policies also generated a number of systemic risks that became all too apparent with the benefit of hindsight. To the extent that the government stood behind bank lending – either explicitly or implicitly – banks themselves did not develop strong risk assessment and management capabilities. Bank lending was misallocated, leaking into speculative activities such as real estate. Debt–equity ratios rose to unsustainable levels, and banks accumulated more and more nonperforming assets, with few institutional or legal mechanisms for resolving them.

In another irony, governments that had – according to the neoclassical consensus – grown largely through exploitation of comparative advantage and market means were now lambasted as exemplars of inefficient intervention and crony capitalism. Defenders of the developmental state model told a very different story about the crisis, emphasizing that it could be traced precisely to deregulation, and capital account and financial market liberalization in particular (Chang 1998; Wade and Veneroso 1998; Amsden 2001, ch. 9; Stiglitz 2002). Yet whatever its origins, the crisis resulted in another round of external pressures for liberalization, particularly in those countries that were constrained to borrow from the IMF.

5.1.3 The Deepening of International Production Networks

Finally, it is important to take note of the dramatic expansion of international production networks in East Asia. The developmental state literature focused primarily on the policies pursued by governments and the political foundations of national growth strategies. Yet another strand of highly influential political economy was looking at the East Asian experience through the lens of these deepening networks.[36] This focus was underplayed by early developmental state analysis of Japan and Korea since both countries

---

[36] This literature is vast, so I focus here on influential treatments that engaged – sometimes in explicit opposition – to the developmental state approach. Gary Gereffi stands out (Gereffi and Wyman 1990; Gereffi and Korzeniewicz 1994; Gereffi 1999; Gereffi, Humphrey, and Sturgeon 2005), particularly for highlighting the difference between producer- and buyer-driven production networks in the region. Doner 1991 was one of the earliest industry studies of the region by a political scientist. Borrus, Ernst, and Haggard 2000 considered the differences among US, Japanese, Taiwanese, and Korean networks. Baldwin 1997 and a myriad of studies that followed tied production networks to Asia's regionalization. Ernst focused early on the relationship between production networks and the diffusion of technological capabilities (for example, Ernst and Kim 2002), a theme of obvious relevance to the developmental state approach. The framework proposed by Henderson et al. 2002 in an influential article, by contrast, explicitly sought to break with "state-centered" analysis of which the developmental state literature was obviously an exemplar. An interesting effort to combine an economic approach to the developmental state with an appreciation of global production networks is Feenstra and Hamilton 2006. For a more recent review that focuses on upgrading, of obvious relevance to the developmental state literature, see Pipkin and Fuentes 2018.

sought to limit foreign investment in favor of national champions; Amsden went so far as to identify such controls as a core element of the model. Yet Taiwan was more open to FDI than Korea, and as the export-oriented growth model migrated south, foreign direct investment became more and more central to rapid export growth. Singapore was identified early as a case in which industrialization was built almost entirely around attraction of foreign firms.[37] Although some expressed skepticism whether such investment could be the pathway for the next tier of flying geese to move up the regional value chain (for example, Bernard and Ravenhill 1995), there could be little doubt that these networks had become a ubiquitous feature of the region's political economy. As we will see, the rebirth of developmental state ideas was of necessity pre-occupied with how to maximize local returns from participation in these networks, and to both capital and labor in the host countries (Pipkin and Fuentes 2017).

In sum, developmental states emerged in a particularly permissive international context, in which both the geostrategic and economic interests of the advanced industrial states provided space for their aggressively export-oriented growth strategies. Over time, however, binding trade commitments, pressures for liberalization, and the growth of international production networks fundamentally changed the external environment.

- Rather than having room for selective protection and controls on FDI, trade and investment policies were constrained to be relatively open.
- Exchange rate policy, which had been calibrated by the developmental states to support exports, came under closer scrutiny.
- While the WTO Agreement on Subsidies and Countervailing Measures provided some scope for general subsidies – including with respect to R&D – other subsidies that were the bread

---

[37] In Akamatsu-like fashion, the first tier of developmental states themselves became the source of foreign investment in manufacturing, starting with Japan but ultimately spreading to Korea, Taiwan, and Singapore (Borrus, Ernst, and Haggard 2000).

and butter of industrial policy were constrained by WTO disciplines.[38]

- Activities of state-owned enterprises also fell under closer scrutiny as did strategic pricing strategies on the part of private firms that fell under dumping statute.

As the discussion of technology in Section 3 has already suggested, a new generation of work on the developmental state was already considering how it operated in a more open-economy context, with a particular focus on the problem of industrial upgrading (Weiss 1998; Deyo, Doner, and Hershberg 2001; Yusuf 2003; Low 2004; Rodrik 2007; Wong 2004, 2011; Doner 2009; Hayashi 2010). But in the wake of the global financial crisis, this discussion was joined in a much larger stream of work on so-called middle-income traps set in train by Gill and Kharas (2007).[39]

5.2 Middle-Income Traps and the New Economics of Industrial Policy

The puzzle of possible middle-income traps was initially posed by a longer-run observation: that of 101 middle-income economies in 1960, only 13 had graduated to high-income status by 2008, with the East Asian developmental states and a handful of early entrants into the EU dominating the list.[40] But the timing of the Gill and

---

[38] Export and local-content subsidies are prohibited outright but a variety of "specific" subsidies are also actionable. The basic principle is that a subsidy that distorts the allocation of resources within an economy should be subject to discipline. The concept of specificity includes enterprise-, industry-, and regional-specific subsidies. See WTO, "Agreement on Subsidies and Countervailing Measures ("SCM Agreement")" at www.wto.org/english/tratop_e/scm_e/subs_e.htm.

[39] The literature is now vast. See Gill and Kharas 2015; and Doner and Schneider 2016 for reviews from an economic and political viewpoint respectively. A related strand of work asked whether middle-income countries were themselves experiencing "premature deindustrialization" (Tan 2013 on Malaysia; Rodrik 2015). For a review of approaches from a global value-chain perspective see Pipkin and Fuentes 2017.

[40] In addition to Japan, Korea, Taiwan, Hong Kong, and Singapore, the list includes Greece, Ireland, Portugal, and Spain and a heterogeneous group of Israel, Puerto Rico, Mauritius, and Equitorial Guinea, an oil-state anomaly.

Kharas piece gave these observations new force. Their analysis appeared just before the global financial crisis of 2008 struck, generating deep-seated anxiety that the period of unusually high growth in the emerging markets over the 2000s was coming to an end. Several critics challenged the very concept of the middle-income trap, noting that high-growth episodes were always vulnerable to regression to the mean (Easterly et al. 1993; Pritchett and Summers 2014). But whether there were identifiable middle-income traps was not altogether relevant to the underlying political anxiety: that growth in many middle-income countries was slowing and new policy initiatives might be needed to meet rising social expectations.

Gill and Kharas argued that more standard trade- and financial-sector reforms still remained relevant for avoiding the middle-income trap. But they made two concessions that showed that industrial policy was back on the table. First, they claimed that "there is some support for the notion that industrial policy becomes more important in middle-income countries in managing the transition to greater technological sophistication" (Gill and Kharas 2015, 12). It is widely known that middle-income countries not only invest much less in R&D than high-income countries but that they frequently underinvest in R&D compared to what would be predicted on the basis of their income per capita alone (Doner and Schneider 2016, 9). This deficit left open space not only for parametric policy reforms, for example with respect to intellectual property rights, but also greater state investment and targeted promotion of innovation.

The second area where Gill and Kharas conceded an opening for industrial policy was in the transition to higher-level skills in the workforce. East Asia's developmental states had done well in expanding education in advance of their takeoff. They had also moved adeptly into high-quality vocational training and investment into the so-called STEM (science, technology, engineering, and math) fields that were complementary to innovation and upgrading. With other policy instruments limited, the expansion of skills became even more paramount than it had been in the past.

Following Sen (1999), Evans and Heller (2015) went so far as to argue that the expansion of capabilities was the essence of the twenty-first-century developmental state, and particularly in democratic settings as we will see in more detail later in this section. These assertions fit not only with the new or endogenous growth theory but with a wealth of new empirical work showing that human development was an antecedent rather than an outcome of economic growth, including in the East Asian developmental states (Ranis, Stuart and Ramirez 2000; Hanushek and Wussman 2008).

Showing how policies for industrial upgrading and the expansion of skills might work across a range of industries facing vastly different challenges is impossible. The challenge of drawing lessons is compounded by the growing recognition that industrial policies cannot simply be focused on the promotion of manufactured exports. However significant they remain to developmentalist thinking (see for example Paus 2012a), the relevance of industrial policy will increasingly hinge on the ability to extend interventionist ideas to activities that face quite different challenges. These range from agriculture and extractive industries to the service sector, which typically accounts for the bulk of economic output in both advanced and developing countries alike.

Yet some general principles drawn from the earlier developmental state experience remain important. As we saw in the discussion of technology, upgrading is particularly dependent on state capacity, not simply in understanding the demands of particular industries but in coordinating among a variety of actors: investors, domestic investors, universities, labs, skilled workers, unions, and even NGOs. Increasingly, such coordination demands an understanding of global production networks as well, and how local industries fit into them (Pipkin and Fuentes 2017), Indeed, as I emphasized in Section 2, it is this *institutional* dimension of industrial policy that is as significant as the particular policy instruments themselves.

Rodrik (2007) explains this way of thinking about industrial policy most clearly. His summary comes straight out of the conception of the growth process as demanding solution to a succession of ever-shifting collective action problems:

> The task of industrial policy is as much about eliciting information from the private sector on significant externalities and their remedies as it is about implementing appropriate policies. The right model for industrial policy is not that of an autonomous government applying Pigovian taxes or subsidies, but of strategic collaboration between the private sector and the government with the aim of uncovering where the most significant obstacles to restructuring lie and what type of interventions are most likely to remove them. (3)

Rodrik goes on to argue that industrial policy should be seen as a process, a finding that is also mirrored in a number of more policy-oriented "how to" manuals. For example, in their call for a revival of industrial policy in Latin America, Devlin and Moguillansky (2011) begin by talking about the importance of constructing "alliances." They define such alliances as "a 'bridging tool' that can bond different intersectoral interests into a common vision for collective action that mobilizes a country's fullest capacity for the cause of economic transformation" (81). They pay particular attention to the institutional arrangements for sustaining such alliances in a number of advanced industrial and Asian as well as Latin American cases (79–104; Melo and Rodriguez-Clare 2006 on "productive development policies" in Latin America).

Similar institutional and organizational issues arise in the context of developing educational and training policies that will be relevant to firms. Kharas and Gill (2015), 12) state the puzzle by asking whether the "appropriate strategy [is] to increase the supply of higher education [and vocational training] with the prior belief that better jobs will follow, or to create jobs and hope that supply adapts to labor market conditions." Yet the challenges again center less on policy than how to orchestrate the complex organizations that constitute the supply-and-demand side of the educational marketplace. As Doner and Schneider (2016, 9) put it, training and employing more technical personnel requires both "extensive horizontal coordination among private firms, research institutes, and universities to create the new positions and develop specialized curricula, as well as massive vertical coordination among the thousands of teachers and students who will implement the new training and education programs."

If we see the importance of institutions for collective action as at the core of the developmental state, we are of necessity back on the terrain of politics as much as economics; it is to these challenges that I now turn.

5.3 The New Political Economy of the Developmental State: State Capacity and Social Coalitions in Democratic Context

Beginning in the mid-1980s, the canonical Northeast Asian developmental states – Korea and Taiwan – democratized, followed with a lag by democratization or at least liberalization in a number of the Southeast Asian countries including Thailand, Indonesia, and Malaysia. Yet these changes were only exemplary of a broader global process: the dramatic expansion of the number of democracies that occurred from 1975 through the present. To be sure, this move toward more liberal politics is by no means consolidated, and backsliding has occurred in a number of major middle-income countries, from Poland and Turkey to the Philippines and Thailand. Moreover, there is the looming question of whether the Chinese model of authoritarian growth may ultimately have transnational appeal. Nonetheless, authoritarian rule cannot be considered the political default setting for industrial policy making, as was true in earlier developmental states outside Japan. If industrial policy is to work, it now needs to do so in a democratic setting.

As with the "classic" developmental state literature, the political foundations start with capable states. In an indictment of contemporary approaches to governance, Francis Fukuyama (2013; 2016) argues that both academics and the policy community have placed too much emphasis on the role of regime type, institutions of accountability, and the rule of law and not enough on state autonomy and capacity. Although cast modestly as an exercise in measurement, Fukuyama circles back to long-standing themes in the developmental state literature and the very different political institutions on which that work focused.

Fukuyama (2013, 4) seeks to redefine governance as "a government's ability to make and enforce rules and to deliver services." Procedural features of bureaucratic organization might matter in this regard, such as the "Weberian-ness" of bureaucratic recruitment and organization. But Fukuyama is drawn to measures of capacity rooted ultimately in the quality and professionalization of personnel and bureaucratic autonomy. Although Fukuyama draws his inspiration from Samuel Huntington, the link to the developmental state tradition and to Johnson in particular could not be more obvious. Autonomy for Fukuyama is the extent to which principals – the politicians – are willing to empower bureaucracies – the agents – by providing broad mandates. However, he explicitly links the likely success of such delegation to factors that motivated Evans as well:

> An appropriate degree of bureaucratic autonomy does not mean that bureaucrats should be isolated from their societies or make decisions at odds with citizen demands. Indeed, if the general mandate is to provide high-quality services in health or education, the bureaucracy would need considerable feedback and criticism from the citizens that it is trying to serve. It also does not exclude extensive collaboration with private sector or civil society organizations in service delivery. Indeed, an appropriately autonomous bureaucracy should be able to make judgment calls as to when and where to engage in such collaborations. (11)

Fukuyama concludes that the quality of government ultimately resides at the intersection of autonomy and capacity. He does not develop a theory about how such a sweet spot might be hit, but he does argue that the optimal level of autonomy is dependent on capacity, with low-capacity states requiring more intrusive monitoring than high-capacity ones. In his most controversial claim, Fukuyama argues that at lower levels of development there are higher returns from increasing state capacity than there are from designing checks. This expectation has been supported in at least one empirical study of the issue by Hanson (2014). He finds that at low levels of development, measures of basic state authority have larger effects on the growth of the capital stock and productivity than measures of checks. Again, this is a finding that is wholly consonant with the developmental state tradition, but which cuts against rule-of-law models (as well as democratic aspirations). In any case, debates about state capacity and how to conceptualize and measure it are clearly back and will be a significant research stream going forward (Hendrix 2010; Besley and Persson 2011; Rothstein and Teorell 2012; Bersch, Praca, and Taylor 2017).

By far the more complicated question is how to think about the coalitional foundations of successful economic development. Democratization meant that any consideration of policy needed to include the play of electoral and legislative politics and thus of political parties, a theme that only the developmental state writing on Japan had fully recognized (for example, Noble 1998). This question opened onto the very much broader one of the conditions under which new democracies could forge programmatic as opposed to clientelistic parties (for example, Kitschelt and Kselman 2013). Democratization also implied fundamental changes in relationships with key social actors. Political liberalization and democratization not only created political opportunities for labor and other civil society actors but opened the space for the private sector to engage in politics in new ways as well. Under strong developmental states, governments had the instruments to impose discipline on the private sector and align interests.[41] Would democracy provide a new political foundation for doing so, or would it open the door to the capture and rent-seeking that Amsden and other proponents of the developmental

---

[41] A number of studies pointed out that the Asian financial crisis could be attributed at least in part not to overregulation and state intervention but rather to the declining ability of governments to check rent-seeking, the socialization of risk, moral hazard, and outright corruption (Haggard 2000; MacIntyre 2003).

state saw as the fundamental political challenge of long-run growth?

Before turning to some possible paths forward, it is crucial to appreciate the structural headwinds many developing countries face. In a cautionary tale, Ben Schneider's *Hierarchical Capitalism in Latin America* (2013) builds on the varieties of capitalism literature to draw quite pessimistic conclusions for the region, showing how institutional complementarities can combine to impede effective industrial strategies as well as advance them. The prevalence of foreign investment and large diversified groups in the region has historically been coupled with tolerance for highly segmented labor markets, inequality, and a corresponding corporate disinterest in skills development. Moreover, these features of the system constituted a political equilibrium, reinforced by political systems that favored elites and insiders. Generalizing the argument, Doner and Schneider (2016) outline how inequality, the persistence of informality, and firm strategies relying on unskilled labor can easily combine to block more progressive developmentalist coalitions. Their conclusion is sweeping: "that strong upgrading coalitions have not emerged in today's middle-income countries" (12).

Yet if the varieties-of-capitalism approach has taught us anything, it is precisely that there are multiple political and social equilibria that can support long-run convergence toward higher incomes. The new democratic context quickly generated a debate on what a "democratic developmental state" might look like (Robinson and White 1998; Evans 2010. Evans and Heller (2015) are exemplary of this new thinking, starting with the very metrics of what we consider "development" to be. Whereas earlier developmental state literature had focused on the standard measure of development as the growth in output, Evans and Heller followed Sen (1999) by emphasizing the expansion of human capabilities. In effect, Evans and Heller reconceptualize social policy as existing not in a trade-off with growth-oriented policies, but as a principal means to growth itself.[42] Given that the sacrifices in human rights

---

[42] For recent examples from the United States, see Irwin (2017).

and democracy by earlier developmental states are clearly not acceptable in most middle-income countries, Evans' concept of "embeddedness" took on an entirely new meaning. Not only does the state need network connections with key firms, it needs network connections with a wider array of social forces in civil society in order to advance the development of human capital, including health, education and the specific skills that would bring at least portions of the private sector on board.

What political alliances might permit such a win-win outcome? Evans, Huber, and Stephens (2017) remind us of at least the possibility of the Northern European social democratic model, and Huber and Stephens (2012) show its effect on social policy and inequality in Latin America. But Sandbrook et al. (2007) take the case directly to the issue of long-run growth as well, showing how four small open economies – Costa Rica, Chile, Mauritius, and the state of Kerala in India – managed to forge consensus around developmentalist projects in democratic settings. Social democratic parties and coalitions figure centrally in their argument, although not necessarily based on strong working class movements; they note that small farmers, white-collar employees, and small business played a political role as well. Sandbrook et al. admit that the structural conditions for the emergence of social democracy on the periphery are narrow and demanding.[43] They nonetheless show how the triumph of moderate left parties created the political foundations for open-economy strategies that produced strong economic performance along with equitable social outcomes. Crucial to this outcome: a capable "social-democratic developmental state" (see also Brautigam 1997 on Mauritius).

Another collective research project (Paus 2012a) reaches similar "possibilitistic" conclusions. Paus and her colleagues show how Chile, the Dominican Republic, Jordan, and Ireland as well as Singapore escaped the middle-income trap, in part through

---

[43] Their argument combines early incorporation into global markets based on small-holder agriculture and the subsequent alignment of agriculture and the bourgeoisie around democracy. They also emphasize favorable colonial legacies that – not surprisingly – contributed to strong states.

successful incorporation into global production networks. The project makes the case for successful state intervention and the development of underlying capacity, but in a way that shows the complementarity between social policy and upgrading highlighted by Evans and Heller:

> The country analyses demonstrate that strategic, proactive, and coherent government policies for capability advancement are a key determinant of upgrading in open economies, both at the country level and in the development of "pockets of excellence." The studies suggest that advancement of social capabilities without development of firm level capabilities does not generate broadbased upgrading. Conversely, insufficient development of social capabilities limits the upgrading possibilities of local firms and the ability of TNC affiliates to move up the value chain within the company's global network. (Paus 2012a, 138)

The political foundations of this successful approach are less clearly theorized, but the cases provide compelling hints. Paus' (2012b) own contribution on Ireland, for example, comports with other studies (for example, Riain 2014) in showing that the successful phase of institutional development occurred under a left-of-center "Rainbow Coalition" from 1994–1997, and included tight linkages between state agencies, universities, research institutes, and the private sector. When this coalition fell apart, the Fianna Fáil-Progressive Democrat coalition pursued more neoliberal policies favoring financialization and overinvestment in real estate, setting the stage for the subsequent financial crisis.

The suggestion that social democratic or center-left coalitions may be more favorable to developmentalist policies is far from established, and there are no doubt other possibilities ranging from more narrow pro-business coalitions to those engaging civil society actors (Evans, Huber, and Stephens 2017). But it is important to underscore that the developmental state literature did not focus solely on the national level but on particular industries – for example, electronics (Evans 1995), – regions (Penang), or both, as in Doner's (2009) analysis of Thailand. Indeed, a powerful literature set in train by Piore and Sabel (1984), Saxenian (1994), Cooke (2001), and others has identified the operation of public–private networks at the regional level as the most promising avenue for generating innovation, and indeed as the way that it typically takes place. As Cooke (2001, 961) puts it, in language that could have come straight out of Evans, "the embedded region will display inclusivity, monitoring, consultation, delegation and networking propensities among its policymakers while the disembedded region will have organizations that tend to be exclusive, reactive, authoritarian and hierarchical." It is most likely that successful coordination will form around particular industries or regions that already show signs of internationalization, clustering, and innovation. Some of these success stories of cross-class coalition formation around product and skill upgrading at the industry or subnational level are surprising: Cammett's (2007) comparative study of upgrading in Morocco and Tunisia in the textile and apparel industry; McDermott's (2007) study of the Argentine wine industry; Shranck's (2011) analysis of the diffusion of modular production strategies in the Dominican garment industry; Heller's (2017) study of urban governance in India, Brazil, and South Africa and the wider review by Pipkin and Fuentes (2017). All underline that the developmental state tradition is not limited to analysis of whole countries, but can be repurposed to understand the institutional and coalitional foundations of upgrading at the sectoral and regional level as well.

5.4   The Return of the Developmental State

Before turning in the conclusion to some broader conclusions, it is important here to restate the modest sociology of knowledge that this section has tried to cover. By the end of the 1980s, it appeared that a set of international and domestic political changes – both material and ideational – had rendered the developmental state an historical relic. Particularly significant in this regard were changes on the international economic front that were inducing liberalization and limiting the instruments that developing countries could deploy: protection, financial crises, and the growth of production networks. But in the wake of the global financial crisis, ideological winds shifted and concerns about the middle-income trap reinvigorated discussion of how to attack bottlenecks in the growth process, particularly with respect to R&D, upgrading, and skills development. Industrial policy was back on the table. Even if the developmental state could not be replicated *in toto*, targeted, sectoral, and regional initiatives to foster growth and innovation seemed plausible.

Developments on the political front also seemed to limit the applicability of the developmental state model. But transitions to democratic rule hardly dampened demand for growth-promoting policies; they simply changed the political circumstances in which those demands arose. Skills and learning more broadly were always central features of the developmental state model. Why couldn't these elements be reconfigured in a democratic context? What were the coalitions that might support such policy innovations? And how could institutional arrangements be devised to solve coordination problems, even if through different means? Some tentative answers to these enduring problems are offered by way of conclusion.

6 The Developmental State Is Dead: Long Live the Developmental State!

Scrutiny of the remarkable growth performance of the East Asian developmental states proved a fertile undertaking. By exploring these growth outliers, light was cast on a host of more general problems in the political economy of development, from how to design effective industrial policy to the political foundations of long-run growth. What we learned did not take the form of formal models or lawlike generalizations. The three canonical Northeast Asian cases of Japan, Korea, and Taiwan did not present an easily identified model. Nonetheless, casework generated more complex and nuanced findings on the configuration of factors that combined to spur rapid growth.

Complexity is not particularly gratifying. What lessons can we take away? I again cluster them by economic and political findings, with a particular emphasis on the latter because of the paramount role of institutions in the developmental state story. I also close with a word about method and the advantages of local knowledge.

The first general finding goes to the heart of how we view development. Rather than the macro processes identified in neoclassical growth models, the alternative canon sees growth through a micro lens as a succession of ever-changing coordination problems. Sometimes markets and private actors are perfectly capable of solving these coordination problems, as in the just-so general equilibrium world. But the presumption that market solutions are always and everywhere superior not only defies common sense, but blithely ignores the multiple assumptions required for this picture of the world to operate: well-functioning markets of all sorts, including financial and insurance markets; good if not perfect information; the absence of serious externalities; an appropriate political economy with sharply delineated and defended property rights. These are conditions that more closely approximate a country that is *already* developed rather than one that is poor and developing. In any case, the findings about the effectiveness of industrial policies in solving these coordination problems are conditional ones: not that industrial policy is necessarily superior to a laissez-faire counterfactual but that in a second-best world with substantial market imperfections it *can* be and that serious thought should be given to the conditions under which it is.

A second lesson that comes out of this review is a negative one: the slaying of a stereotype. The phrase "picking winners" has become a particularly unhelpful trope for understanding how industrial policy worked in East Asia. The idea that East Asia was blessed by an omniscient, far-seeing, and welfare-enhancing state has given rise to the injunction that such states are rare and that prudence justifies an abstemious approach to government intervention. But even the abbreviated vignettes presented here suggest that the process of forging effective industrial policies was just that – a process. It did not involve insulated bureaucrats "picking winners," but rather political institutions that facilitated coordination among states and private actors engaged in an iterative process of learning.

These observations, central to the view of the development process held by Amsden, Evans, and Rodrik, lead immediately to questions of political economy. A third conclusion from the developmental state literature has to do with state capacity. The new institutional economics approach to long-run growth focuses on checks on the executive, the rule of law, and the protection of property rights and contracting. Yet even performing night-watchman state functions requires state capacity: courts, regulators, and bureaucracies that function and personnel in them that are adequately incentivized or socialized to the provision of public goods. The significance of capacity is not necessarily denied in liberal and new institutional economics accounts of growth. Yet neither is it emphasized, and as I underline in Section 5 this lacuna is deafening. We know a lot more about how to design an exchange rate regime than we do about making bureaucracies in poor countries work.

A fourth conclusion has to do with the social foundations of long-run growth. The caricature of the developmental state is that it rested on a social foundation of authoritarian rule (or dominant party rule in the case of Japan), close ties to business, and the subordination of labor. The reality is significantly more nuanced, starting with how states interacted with the private sector, as we have just seen. One of the biggest ironies of the developmental state venture was that it ultimately had a greater appreciation of the dynamics and costs of rent-seeking than its neoclassical adversaries. Among the pioneers of the neoclassical approach to East Asia's growth were economists who made first-rate theoretical contributions to our understanding of rent-seeking, most notably Krueger (1974) and Bhagwati (1982). Yet their explanations for Asia's success lacked a political economy of the transition to high growth and how pervasive rent-seeking was overcome.

Moreover, the effects of rents depend mightily on the nature of the political quid pro quo between states and capitalist classes. States that fall wholly under the sway of the private sector are not going to be market-oriented ones; to the contrary. "Discipline" of business, permitted by states capable of controlling capture and access and eliciting information, played a key role in the developmental state story. Nor is this theme limited to the developmental state literature. It is visible, for example, in Rajan and Zingales' (2004) aptly titled book on the necessity of "saving capitalism from the capitalists." Simply stated, effective economic policy *of any sort* rests on constraining private power and imposing discipline on private actors. The developmental state work shows that such discipline was not only necessary for effective industrial policy but for transitions toward more market-oriented policies as well.

Nor is the story of labor subordination altogether straightforward. To be sure, authoritarian developmental states were right-wing dictatorships that controlled labor organization both in the polity as a whole and down to the shop floor. Yet developmental states also rested on complementary investments in human capital that proved a critical input to the growth process.

As we think about economic policy in democratic settings, the question of how to forge cross-class coalitions for growth has once again become an agenda for research, including the question of how to assure continuing investment in human capabilities. The varieties of capitalism literature has taught us that there is no one route to success; Europe converged with the United States in the postwar period pursuing a variety of distinctive economic models (Hall and Soskice 2001). However, we can say that growth itself needs to be undergirded by some coalition of support, even if variable and shifting. Policy failures can frequently be traced to stalemates, conflicts, or fragmented interests that do not cohere.

Lastly, a word on method and social purpose. A striking feature of developmental state research was deep engagement with history, path dependencies, and cases. We are once again seeing important debates about method in the social sciences, spurred in part by a very particular definition of causal inference rooted in experimental models. However, growth is a macro phenomenon, and unless we eschew such work altogether – as some purists have argued – we are stuck with making sense of history. It is refreshing that even within economics there are some voices calling into question the new methodological orthodoxy and noting the importance of contextualization (for example Deaton and Cartwright 2016). There are even more spirited discussions within political science about the advantages of mixed methods, within case-causal inference and comparative historical analysis.[44] There is certainly room for more cross-national comparative work on the varieties of developing country capitalism and state formation (Centeno, Kohli, and Yashar with Mistree 2017). The lessons of the developmental state literature are not just theoretical and empirical, but also a reminder of how good comparative history can be done.

Which brings me finally to purpose. How was this history to be used? Some strands of the new institutionalism in economics (Acemoglu, Johnson, and Robinson 2001) reached implicitly pessimistic conclusions about the capacity to escape poverty traps, noting the heavy weight of the dead hand of history. The developmental state literature by contrast was from its inception deeply motivated by an engagement with policy debates. Wade, Amsden, Chang, Evans, Rodrik, and others were not simply historians of development but pragmatists wary of cookie-cutter models and on the lookout for good ideas. Deterministic formulations on the origins of long-run growth – including some of those that lurked in the developmental state literature itself – were ultimately of less interest to them than mining history for lessons that could be adapted to different national contexts.

---

[44] This literature is too vast to cite here, but two recent overviews are Mahoney and Thelen 2015 on comparative historical approaches and Goertz 2017 on the method of within-case causal inference, both of which are directly relevant to the developmental state approach.

This inductive approach has disabilities to be sure. What is the model? What are the empirical generalizations in which we can have some statistical confidence? These questions reflect a somewhat constricted conception of how knowledge arises, however, not only among analysts but among actors themselves. Those politicians and bureaucrats seeking to produce growth are looking at cases – namely their own – and trying to figure out how to move forward. Induction has become a dirty word, and particularly when cases are selected on the dependent variable of success. But note how we simultaneously think that "best practice" is something that successful companies – and countries – should emulate. If we don't know what the "best practice" was – the range of possibilities – it's hard to draw lessons from it. Local knowledge matters not only for those in the policy fray but for those in the academy trying to understand it.

References

Acemoglu, Daron, Simon Johnson, and James A. Robinson (2001). The colonial origins of comparative development: an empirical investigation. *American Economic Review* 91(5), 1369–1401.

(2005). Institutions as the fundamental cause of long-run growth. In P. Aghion and S. Durlauf, eds., *Handbook of Economic Growth, Vol. 1A.* Amsterdam: North-Holland, pp. 386–472.

Acemoglu, Daron and James A. Robinson (2012) *Why Nations Fail: The Origins of Power, Prosperity, and Poverty.* New York: Crown Group.

Aggarwal, Vinod (1983). *Liberal Protectionism: The International Politics of Organized Textile Trade.* Berkeley, CA: University of California Press.

Akamatsu Kaname. (1962). A historical pattern of economic growth in developing countries. *Journal of Developing Economies* 1(1), 3–25.

Alchian, Armen. (1965). Some economics of property rights. *Il Politico* 30(4), 816–829.

Alchian, Armen., and Harold Demsetz (1973). The property rights paradigm. *Journal of Economic History* 33(1), 16–27.

Amsden, Alice (1989). *Asia's Next Giant: South Korea and Late Industrialization.* New York, NY: Oxford University Press.

(1991). Diffusion of development: the late-industrializing model and greater East Asia. *The American Economic Review* 81(2), 282–286.

(1994). Why isn't the whole world experimenting with the East Asian model to develop? Review of The East Asian Miracle. *World Development* 22(4), 627–633.

(2001). *The Rise of "the Rest": Challenges to the West from Late-Industrializing Economies.* New York, NY: Oxford University Press.

Amsden, Alice, and Wan Wen Chu (2003). *Beyond Late Development: Taiwan's Upgrading Policies.* Cambridge, MA: MIT Press.

Anchordoguy, Marie (1989). *Computers Inc.: Japan's Challenge to IBM.* Cambridge: Harvard Council on East Asian Studies.

96

Aoki, Masahiko, Hyung-Ki Kim, and Masahiro Okuno-Fujiwara, eds. (1997). *The Role of Government in East Asian Economic Development: Comparative Institutional Analysis.* New York, NY: Oxford University Press.

Appelbaum, Richard P., and Jeffrey Henderson, eds. (1992). *States and Development in the Asian Pacific Rim.* Newbury Park, CA: Sage Publications.

Autor, David H., David Dorn, and Gordon Hanson (2013). The China syndrome: local labor market effects of import competition in the United States. *American Economic Review* 103 6), 2121–2168.

Baek, Seung-wook (2005). Does China follow "the East Asian Development Model"? *Journal of Contemporary Asia* 35(4), 485–498.

Bairoch, Paul (1972). Free trade and European economic development in the 19th century. *European Economic Review* 3(3), 211–245.

(1993). *Economics and World History: Myths and Paradoxes.* Chicago, IL: University of Chicago Press.

Balassa, Bela (1981). *The Newly Industrializing Countries in the World Economy.* New York, NY: Pergamon Press.

Baldwin, David, and Paul Krugman (1988). Market access and competition: a simulation study of 16K random access memories. In Robert Feenstra, ed., *Empirical Models for Industrial Trade.* Cambridge, MA: MIT Press, pp. 171–197.

Baldwin, Robert (1997). The causes of regionalism. *The World Economy* 20(7), 865–888.

Barzel, Yoram (1997). *Economic Analysis of Property Rights*, 2nd edition. New York, NY: Cambridge University Press.

Bernard, Michael and John Ravenhill (1995). Beyond product cycles and flying geese regionalization, hierarchy, and the industrialization of East Asia. *World Politics* 47(2), 171–209.

Bersch, Katherine, Sergio Praca, and Matthew M. Taylor (2017). Bureaucratic capacity and political autonomy within national states: mapping the archipelago of excellence in Brazil. In Miguel Centeno, Atul Kohli, and Deborah Yashar with Dinish Mistree, eds., *States in the Developing World.* New York, NY: Cambridge University Press, pp. 157–183.

Besley, Timothy, and Maitreesh Ghatak (2010). Property rights and economic development. In Dani Rodrik and Mark Rosenzweig, eds., *Handbook of Development Economics, Vol. 5.* Amsterdam: North-Holland, pp. 4525–4595.

Besley, Timothy, and Torsten Persson (2011). *Pillars of Prosperity: The Political Economy of Development Clusters*. Princeton, NJ: Princeton University Press.

Bhagwati, Jagdish (1978). *Foreign Trade Regimes and Economic Development, Vol. 11. Anatomy and Consequences of Exchange Control Regimes*. Cambridge, MA: Ballinger Publishing Co. for the National Bureau of Economic Research.

(1982). Directly unproductive, profit-seeking (DUP) activities. *Journal of Political Economy* 90(5), 988–1002.

Bhagwati, Jagdish, and Hugh Patrick, eds. (1991). *Aggressive Unilateralism: America's 301 Policy and the World Trading System*. Ann Arbor, MI: University of Michigan Press.

Birdsall, Nancy, and Francis Fukuyama (2011). The post-Washington consensus: development after the crisis, *Foreign Affairs* March/April.

Birsdsall, Nancy, David Ross, and Richard Sabot (1995). Inequality and growth reconsidered: lessons from East Asia. *The World Bank Economic Review* 9(3), 477–508.

Bluestone, Barry, and Bennet Harrison (1982). *The Deindustrialization of America: Plant Closings, Community Abandonment, and the Dismantling of Basic Industry*. New York, NY: Basic Books.

Borrus, Michael, Dieter Ernst, and Stephan Haggard, eds. (2003). *International Production Networks in Asia: Rivalry or Riches?* New York, NY: Routledge.

Brander, James (1995). Strategic trade policy. In Gene Grossman and Kenneth Rogoff, eds., *Handbook of International Economics, Vol. III*. Amsterdam: Elsevier, pp. 1395–1455.

Brautigam, Deborah (1997). Institutions, economic reform, and democratic consolidation in Mauritius. *Comparative Politics* 30 (1), 45–62.

Calder, Kent E. (1993). *Strategic Capitalism: Private Business and Public Purpose in Japanese Industrial Finance*. Princeton, NJ: Princeton University Press.

Cammett, Melanie (2007). Business–government relations and industrial change: the politics of upgrading in Morocco and Tunisia. *World Development* 35(11), 1889–1903.

Campos, Edgardo J. and Hilton L. Root (1996). *The Key to the Asian Miracle: Making Shared Growth Credible*. Washington, DC: The Brookings Institution.

Centeno, Miguel, Atul Kohli, and Deborah Yashar with Dinish Mistree, eds. (2017). *States in the Developing World.* New York, NY: Cambridge University Press.

Chan, Steve, Cal Clark, and Danny Lam, eds. (1998). *Beyond the Developmental State: East Asia's Political Economies Reconsidered.* New York, NY: St. Martin's Press.

Chan, Sylvia (2002). *Liberalism, Democracy and Development.* New York, NY: Cambridge University Press.

Chang, Ha-Joon (1994). *The Political Economy of Industrial Policy.* Basingstoke: Macmillan.

(1998). Korea: the misunderstood crisis. *World Development* 26(8), 1555–1561.

(2002). *Kicking Away the Ladder: Development Strategy in Historical Perspective.* London: Anthem Press.

Cheng, Tun-Jen. (1990). Political regimes and development strategies: South Korea and Taiwan. In Gary Gereffi and Donald Wyman, eds., *Manufacturing Miracles: Patterns of Development in Latin American and East Asia,* Princeton, NJ: Princeton University Press, pp. 139–178.

(1993). Guarding the commanding heights: the state as banker in Taiwan. In Stephan Haggard, Chung Lee, and Sylvia Maxfield, eds., *The Politics of Finance in Developing Countries.* Ithaca, NY: Cornell University Press, pp. 55–92.

Cheng, Tun-Jen, Stephan Haggard, and David Kang (1998). Institutions and growth in Korea and Taiwan: the bureaucracy. *Journal of Development Studies* 34(6), 87–111.

Chibber, Vivek (2003). *Locked in Place: State-Building and Late Industrialization in India.* Princeton, NJ: Princeton University Press.

(2014). The developmental state in retrospect and prospect: lessons from India and South Korea. In Michelle Williams, ed., *The End of the Developmental State?* London: Routledge, pp. 30–54.

Chiu Stephen Wing-kai, Kong-chong Ho, and Tai-lok Lui (1997). *City-States in the Global Economy: Industrial Restructuring in Hong Kong and Singapore.* Boulder, CO: Westview Press.

Cline, William (1982). Can the East Asian model of growth be generalized? *World Development,* 10 (2), 81–90.

Commission on Growth and Development (2008). *The Growth Report: Strategies for Sustained Growth and Inclusive Development.* Washington, DC: The World Bank.

Cooke, Philip (2001). Regional innovation systems, clusters and the knowledge economy. *Industrial and Corporate Change* 10(4), 945–974.

Cumings, Bruce (1984). The origins and development of the Northeast Asian political economy: industrial sectors, product cycles, and political consequences. *International Organization* 38(1), 1–40.

Dahlman, Carl J. Bruce Ross-Larson and Larry Westphal (1987). Managing technological development: lessons from the newly industrializing countries. *World Development* 15(6), 759–775.

Deaton, Angus, and Nancy Cartwright (2016). Understanding and misunderstanding randomized controlled trials. NBER Working Paper 22595 at www.nber.org/papers/w22595. Cambridge, MA: National Bureau of Economic Research.

Demsetz, Harold. (1967). Toward a theory of property rights. *The American Economic Review*, 57(2), 347–359.

De Schweinitz, Karl Jr. (1964). *Industrialization and Democracy: Economic Necessities and Political Possibilities.* New York, NY: The Free Press of Glencoe, Collier-MacMillan Ltd.

Devlin, Robert, and Graciella Moguillansky (2011). *Breeding Latin American Tigers: Operational Principles for Rehabilitating Industrial Policies.* Santiago: Economic Commission for Latin America.

Deyo, Frederic C. (1981). *Dependent Development and Industrial Order: An Asian Case Study*, New York, NY: Praeger.

 ed. (1987). *The Political Economy of the New Asian Industrialism.* Ithaca, NY: Cornell University Press.

 (1989). *Beneath the Miracle: Labor Subordination in the New Asian Industrialism.* Berkeley, CA: University of California Press.

Deyo, Frederic C., Richard F. Doner and Eric Hershberg, eds. (2001). *Economic Governance and the Challenge of Flexibility in East Asia.* Oxford: Rowman and Littlefield.

Domar, Evsey (1946). Capital expansion, rate of growth, and employment. *Econometrica* 14(2), 137–147.

Doner, Richard F. (1991). *Driving a Bargain: Automobile Industrialization and Japanese Firms in Southeast Asia.* Berkeley, CA: University of California Press.

 (2009). *The Politics of Uneven Development: Thailand's Economic Growth in Comparative Perspective.* New York, NY: Cambridge University Press.

Doner, Richard F., Bryan K. Ritchie, and Dan Slater (2005). Systemic vulnerability and the origins of developmental states: Northeast and Southeast Asia in comparative perspective. *International Organization* 59(2), 327–361.

Doner, Richard F. and Ben Ross Schneider (2016). The middle-income trap: more politics than economics. *World Politics* 68 (4), 608-644.

Dore, Ronald (1986). *Flexible Rigidities: Structural Adjustment in Japan: 1970-1982.* Palo Alto, CA: Stanford University Press, 1986.

Easterly William, Michael Kremer, Lant Pritchett, and Lawrence Summers (1993). Good policy or good luck?: country growth performance and temporary shocks. *Journal of Monetary Economics* 32(3), 459-483.

Edigheji, Omano (2005). A democratic developmental state in Africa? A concept paper. Johannesburg: Centre for Policy Studies Research Report 105.

ed. (2010). *Constructing a Democratic Developmental State in South Africa.* Cape Town: HSRC Press.

Edwards, Sebastian (1993). Openness, trade liberalization, and growth in developing countries. *Journal of Economic Literature* 31(3), 1358-1393.

Ernst, Dieter, and Linsu Kim (2002). Global production networks, knowledge diffusion, and local capability formation. *Research Policy* 31(8-9), 1417-1429.

Evans, Peter (1989). Predatory, developmental and other apparatuses: a comparative political economy perspective on the Third World state. *Sociological Forum* 4(4): 561-587.

(1995). *Embedded Autonomy: States and Industrial Transformation.* Princeton, NJ: Princeton University Press.

(1998). Transferable lessons? Re-examining the institutional prerequisites of East Asian economic policies. *Journal of Developmental Studies* 34(6), 66-86.

(2010). The challenge of 21st century development: building capability-enhancing states. Working Paper for the United National Development Program 2010 "Capacity *Is* Development" Global Event. New York, NY: UNDP.

Evans, Peter, and Patrick Heller (2015). Human development, state transformation, and the politics of the developmental state. In Stephan Leibfried, Evelyne Huber, Matthew Lange, Jonah D. Levy, and John D. Stephens, eds., *The Oxford Handbook of Transformations of the State.* New York, NY: Oxford University Press.

Evans, Peter, Evelyne Huber, and John D. Stephens (2017). The political foundations of state effectiveness. In Miguel Centeno, Atul Kohli, and

Deborah Yashar with Dinish Mistree, eds., *States in the Developing World*. New York, NY: Cambridge University Press, pp. 380–408.

Evans, Peter, and James Rauch (1999). Bureaucracy and growth: a cross-national analysis of the effects of "Weberian" state structures on economic growth. *American Sociological Review* 64(4), 748–765.

Feenstra, Robert C., and Gary Hamilton (2006). *Emergent Economies, Divergent Paths: Economic Organization and International Trade in South Korea and Taiwan*. New York, NY: Cambridge University Press.

Fields, Karl (1995). *Enterprise and the State in Korea and Taiwan*. Ithaca, NY: Cornell University Press.

Findlay, Ronald, and Kevin O'Rourke (2007). *Power and Plenty: Trade, War, and the World Economy in the Second Millennium*. Princeton, NJ: Princeton University Press.

Friedman, David (1988). *The Misunderstood Miracle: Industrial Development and Political Change in Japan*. Ithaca, NY: Cornell University Press.

Fritz, Verena and Alina Rocha Menocal (2006). (Re)building developmental states: from theory to practice. Working Paper No. 274. London: Overseas Development Institute.

Fukuyama, Francis (2013). What is governance? *Governance* 26(3), 347–368.

  (2016). Governance: what do we know and how do we know it? *Annual Review of Political Science* 19, 89–105.

Gallagher, John, and Ronald Robinson (1953). The imperialism of free trade. *The Economic History Review* 6(1), 1–15.

Garon, Sheldon (1987). *The State and Labor in Modern Japan*. Berkeley, CA: University of California Press.

Geddes, Barbara (2003). *Paradigms and Sand Castles: Theory Building and Research Design in Comparative Politics*. Ann Arbor, MI: University of Michigan Press.

Gereffi, Gary (1999). International trade and industrial upgrading in the apparel commodity chain. *Journal of International Economics* 48(1), 37–70.

Gereffi, Gary, John Humphrey, and Timothy Sturgeon (2005). The governance of global value chains. *Review of International Political Economy* 12(1), 78–104.

Gereffi, Gary, and Miguel Korzeniewicz, eds. (1994). *Commodity Chains and Global Capitalism*. Westport, CT: Greenwood Press.

Gereffi, Gary, and Donald L. Wyman, eds. (1990). *Manufacturing Miracles: Paths of Industrialization in Latin America and East Asia.* Princeton, NJ: Princeton University Press.

Gerschenkron, Alexander (1962). Economic backwardness in historical perspective. In Alexander Gerschenkron, ed., *Economic Backwardness in Historical Perspective: A Book of Essays.* New York, NY: Frederick Praeger, pp. 5–30.

Gill, Indermit and Homi Kharas, eds. (2007). *An East Asian Renaissance: Ideas for Economic Growth.* Washington, D.C.: The World Bank.

(2015). The Middle-Income Trap Turns Ten, World Bank Policy Working Paper no. 7403. Washington: The World Bank.

Ginsburg, Tom (2000). Does law matter for economic development? Evidence from East Asia. *Law and Society Review* 34(3), 829–856.

Goertz, Gary (2017). *Multimethod Research, Causal Mechanisms, and Case Studies:An Integrated Approach.* Princeton, NJ: Princeton University Press.

Gold, Thomas (1980). *Dependent Development in Taiwan.* Unpublished PhD dissertation, Harvard University.

Gomez, Terence and Jomo K.S. (1997). *Malaysia's Political Economy: Politics, Patronage and Profits.* New York: Cambridge University Press.

Goodman, Roger and Ito Peng (1996). The East Asian Welfare States: Peripatetic Learning, Adaptive Change, and Nation-Building in Gosta Esping-Andersen, ed. *Welfare States in Transition.* Thousand Oaks, CA: Sage.

Goodman, Roger, Gordon White and Huck-Ju Kwon, eds. (1998). *The East Asian Welfare Model: Welfare Orientalism and the State.* London: Routledge.

Gough, Ian (2001a). Globalization and Regional welfare regimes: the Asian case, *Global Social Policy* 1, (2), 163–189.

Grabowski, Richard (1994). The successful developmental state: where does it come from? *World Development* 22(3), 413–422.

Haggard, Stephan (1990). *Pathways from the Periphery: The Politics of Growth in the Newly Industrializing Countries.* Ithaca, NY: Cornell University Press.

(2000). *The Political Economy of the Asian Financial Crisis.* Washington, DC: The Institute for International Economics.

(2004). Institutions and growth in East Asia. *Studies in Comparative International Development*, 138(4): 53–81.

(2015). The developmental state is dead: long live the developmental state! In James Mahoney and Kathy Thelen, eds., *Advances in Comparative Historical Analysis.* New York, NY: Cambridge University Press, pp. 39–66.

Haggard, Stephan, David Kang, and Chung-in Moon (1997). Japanese colonialism and Korean development: a critique. *World Development* 25(6), 867–881.

Haggard, Stephan, and Robert R. Kaufman (2008). *Development, Democracy and Welfare States: Latin America, East Asia and Eastern Europe.* Princeton, NJ: Princeton University Press.

Haggard, Stephan, Byung-kook Kim, and Chung-in Moon (1991). The transition to export-led growth in South Korea: 1954–1966. *The Journal of Asian Studies* 50(4), 850–873.

Haggard, S., and C. K. Pang (1994). The transition to export-led growth in Taiwan. In Joel D. Aberbach, David Dollar, and Kenneth L. Sokoloff, eds., *The Role of the State in Taiwan's Development,* Armonk, NY: M. E. Sharpe.

Haggard, Stephan, and Lydia Tiede (2011). The rule of law and economic growth: where are we? *World Development* 39(5), 673–685.

Haggard, Stephan and Yu Zheng (2013). Institutional innovation and private investment in Taiwan: the microfoundations of the developmental state. *Business and Politics* 15(4), 435–46.

Hall, Peter and David Soskice (2001). *Varieties of Capitalism: The Institutional Foundations of Comparative Advantage.* New York: Oxford University Press.

Hamilton, Alexander (1791/1892). *Report on Manufactures.* Boston, MA: The Home Market Club.

Hanson, Jonathan K. (2014). Forging then taming Leviathan: State capacity, constraints on rulers and development. *International Studies Quarterly* 58, 380–392.

Hanushek, Eric A. and Ludger Woessmann (2008). The role of cognitive skills in economic development. *Journal of Economic Literature* 46 (3), 607–668

Harrod, Roy F. (1939). An essay in dynamic theory. *The Economic Journal* 49(193), 14–33.

Hayashi, Shigeko (2010). The developmental state in the era of globalization: beyond the Northeast Asian model of political economy. *The Pacific Review* 23(1), 45–69.

Hecksher, Eli (1931/1994). *Mercantilism.* New York, NY: Routledge.

Heller, Patrick (2017). Development in the city: growth and inclusion in India, Brazil and South Africa. In Miguel Centeno, Atul Kohli, and Deborah Yashar with Dinish Mistree, eds., *States in the Developing World*. New York, NY: Cambridge University Press, pp. 309–338.

Hellman, Thomas, Kevin Murdock, and Joseph Stiglitz (1996). Financial restraint: toward a new paradigm. In Masahiko Aoki, Hyung-Ki Kim, and Masahiro Okuno-Fujiwara, eds., *The Role of Government in East Asian Economic Development: Comparative Institutional Analysis*. New York, NY: Oxford University Press, pp. 163–207.

Henderson, Jeffrey (1993). Against the economic orthodoxy: on the making of the East Asian miracle. *Economy and Society* 22(2), 200–217.

Henderson, Jeffrey, Peter Dicken, Martin Hess, Neil Coe, and Henry Wai-Chung Yeung (2002). Global production networks and the analysis of economic development. *Review of International Political Economy* 9(3), 4436–4464.

Hendrix, Cullen (2010). Measuring state capacity: theoretical and empirical implications for the study of civil conflict. *Journal of Peace Research* 47(3), 273–285.

Herbst, Jeffrey (1990). War and the state in Africa. International Security, 14 (4), 117–139.

Hirschman, Albert (1958). *The Strategy of Economic Development*. New Haven, CT: Yale University Press.

Hobday, M. (1995). *Innovation in East Asia: The Challenge to Japan*. Cheltenham: Edward Elgar.

Holliday, Ian (2000). Productivist welfare capitalism: Social policy in East Asia, *Political Studies* 48, 4 (September): 706-723.

Holliday, Ian and Paul Wilding (2004). *Welfare Capitalism in East Asia: Social Policy in the Tiger Economies*. New York: Palgrave MacMillan.

Huber, Evelyne, and John D. Stephens (2012). *Democracy and the Left: Social Policy and Inequality in Latin America*. Chicago, IL: University of Chicago Press.

Huff, W. G. (1995). The developmental state, government and Singapore's economic development since 1960. *World Development* 23(8), 1421–1438.

Huff, W. G., Gerda Dewit and Christine Oughton (2001). Credibility and reputation building in the developmental state: a model with East Asian applications. *World Development* 29(4), 771–724.

Hughes, Helen, ed. (1988). *Achieving Industrialization in East Asia.* New York, NY: Cambridge University Press.

Huntington, Samuel, and Joan Nelson (1976). *No Easy Choice: Political Participation in Developing Countries.* Cambridge, MA: Harvard University Press.

Im, Hyug Baeg (1987). The rise of bureaucratic authoritarianism in South Korea. *World Politics* 39(2), 231–257.

Irwin, Neil (2017). Supply Side Economics, but for Liberals, *The New York Times,* April 15, 2017 at www.nytimes.com/2017/04/15/upshot/supply-side-economics-but-for-liberals.html.

Jayasuriya, Kanishka (2005). Beyond institutional fetishism: from the developmental to the regulatory state. *New Political Economy* 10(3), 381–387.

Johnson, Chalmers (1978). *Japan's Public Policy Companies.* Washington, DC: American Enterprise Institute.

(1982). *MITI and the Japanese Miracle: The Growth of Industrial Policy, 1925–1975.* Stanford, CA: Stanford University Press.

(1987). Political institutions and economic performance: the government-business relationship in Japan, Korea and Taiwan. In Frederic Deyo, ed., *The Political Economy of the New Asian Industrialism.* Ithaca, NY: Cornell University Press, pp. 136–164.

(1995). *Japan: Who Governs? The Rise of the Developmental State.* New York, NY: W. W. Norton.

(1999). The developmental state: odyssey of a concept. In Meredith Woo-Cumings, ed., *The Developmental State.* Ithaca, NY: Cornell University Press, pp. 32–60.

Jomo, K.S. et. al. (1997). *Southeast Asia's Misunderstood Miracle: Industrial Policy and Economic Development in Thailand, Malaysia and Indonesia.* Boulder: Westview.

Kaldor, Nicholas (1967). *Strategic Factors in Economic Development.* Ithaca, NY: Cornell University Press.

(1971). Conflicts in national objectives. *Economic Journal* 81(321), 1–16.

Kang, David C. (2002a). *Crony Capitalism: Corruption and Development in South Korea and the Philippines.* Cambridge: Cambridge University Press.

(2002b). Money politics and the developmental state in Korea. *International Organization* 56(1), 177–207.

Kasahara, Shigehisa (2013). The Asian Developmental state and the flying geese paradigm, United Nations Conference on Trade and

Development Working Paper No. 213 (November). Geneva: UNCTAD.

Kaufman, Robert R. (1979). Industrial change and authoritarian rule in Latin America: a concrete review of the bureaucratic-authoritarian model. In David Collier, ed., *The New Authoritarianism in Latin America.* Princeton, NJ: Princeton University Press, pp. 165-253.

Kay, Cristobal (1989). *Latin American Theories of Development and Underdevelopment.* Chicago, IL: University of Chicago Press.

Kennedy, Scott (2010). The myth of the Beijing consensus. *Journal of Contemporary China* 19(65), 461-477.

Khan, Moishin. and Jomo K. Sundaram, eds. (2000). *Rents, Rent-Seeking and Economic Development: Theory and the Asian Evidence.* Cambridge: Cambridge University Press.

Kim, Byung-kook (1988). *Bringing and Managing Socioeconomic Change: The State in Korea and Mexico.* Unpublished PhD dissertation, Harvard University.

Kim, Eun Mee (1997). *Big Business, Strong State: Collusion and Conflict in South Korean Development 1960-1990.* Albany, NY: State University of New York Press.

Kim, Jong-Iland Lawrence J. Lau (1994). The sources of economic growth in the East Asian newly industrializing countries. *Journal of Japanese and International Economics* 8(2), 235-271.

Kim, Linsu (1997). *Imitation to Innovation: The Dynamics of Korea's Technological Learning.* Boston, MA: Harvard Business School Press.

Kitschelt, Herbert and Daniel Kselman (2012). Economic development, democratic experience and political parties' linkage strategies. *Comparative Political Studies* 46(11), 1453-1484

Knight, John (2010). China as a developmental state. CSAE Working Paper WPS/2012-13. Oxford: Oxford University, Centre for the Study of African Economies.

Kohli, Atul (2004). *State-Directed Development: Political Power and Industrialization in the Global Periphery.* Cambridge: Cambridge University Press.

Kojima, K. (1966). A Pacific Economic Community and Asian developing countries. *Hitotsubashi Journal of Economics* 7(1), 17-37.

(2000). The flying geese model of Asian economic development: origin, theoretical extensions, and regional policy implications. *Journal of Asian Economics* 11(4), 375-401.

Korhonen, Pekka. (1994). The theory of the flying geese pattern of development and its interpretation. *Journal of Peace Research* 31(1), 93–108.

Krauss, Ellis, and Michio Muramatsu (1984). Bureaucrats and politicians in policymaking: the case of Japan. *American Political Science Review* 78(1), 126–148.

Krueger, Anne (1974). The political economy of the rent-seeking society. *American Economic Review* 64(3), 291–303.

  (1978). *Foreign Trade Regimes and Economic Development, Vol. 10. Liberalization Attempts and Consequences.* Cambridge, MA: Ballinger Publishing Co. for the National Bureau of Economic Research.

Krugman, Paul (1984). Import protection as export promotion: international competition in the presence of oligopoly and economies of scale. In H. Kierzkowski, ed., *Monopolistic Competition and International Trade.* Oxford: Clarendon Press, pp. 180–193.

  ed. (1986). *Strategic Trade Policy and the New International Economics.* Cambridge, MA: MIT Press.

  (1994). The myth of Asia's miracle. *Foreign Affairs* 73(6), 62–78.

Kuo, Chiang-tian (1995). *Global Competitiveness and Industrial Growth in Taiwan and the Philippines.* Pittsburgh, PA: University of Pittsburgh Press.

Lall, Sanjaya (1996). *Learning from the Asian Tigers: Studies in Technology and Industrial Policy.* New York: St. Martin's Press.

Kwon, Huck-ju (1998). Democracy and the politics of social welfare: a comparative analysis of welfare systems in East Asia, in R. Goodman, G. White, and H. J. Kwon, eds, *The East Asian Welfare Model: Welfare Orientalism and the State*, New York: Routledge, pp. 27–74.

Lawrence, Robert Z. (1984). *Can America Compete?* Washington, DC: The Brookings Institution.

Lee, Jong-Wha. (1996). Government intervention and productivity growth. *Journal of Economic Growth* 1(3), 391–414.

Leftwich, Adrian (1995). Bringing politics back in: towards a model of the developmental state. *Journal of Development Studies* 31(3), 400–427.

Lim, Linda Y. C. (1983). Singapore's success: the myth of the free market economy. *Asian Survey* 23(6): 752–764.

Lin, Justin Yifu (2009). *Economic Development and Transition: Thought, Strategy, and Viability.* Cambridge: Cambridge University Press.

Lin, Justin Yifu, and Célestin Monga (2011). Growth identification and facilitation: the role of the state in the dynamics of structural change. *Development Policy Review*, 29(3), 264–290.

List, Friedrich (1841). *The National System of Political Economy* at http://oll .libertyfund.org/titles/list-the-national-system-of-political-economy.

Little, Ian. M. D., Tibor Scitovsky, and Maurice F. G. Scott (1970). *Industry and Trade in Some Developing Countries*. London: Oxford University Press.

Lockwood, William Wirt (1954). *Economic Development of Japan: Growth and Structural Change*. Princeton, NJ: Princeton University Press.

Low, Linda (1998). *Political Economy in a City-State: Government-Made Singapore*, Singapore: Oxford University Press.

    ed. (2004). *Developmental States: Relevancy, Redundancy or Reconfiguration?* Hauppauge, NY: Nova Science Publishers.

MacIntyre, Andrew, ed. (1994). *Business and Government in Industrializing Asia*. Ithaca, NY: Cornell University Press.

    (2003). *The Power of Institutions: Political Architecture and Governance*. Ithaca, NY: Cornell University Press.

Mahoney, James, and Kathy Thelen, eds. (2015). *Advances in Comparative Historical Analysis*. New York, NY: Cambridge University Press.

Maxfield, Sylvia, and Schneider, Ben Ross, eds. (1997). *Business and the State in Developing Countries*. Ithaca, NY: Cornell University Press.

McDermott, Gerald A. (2007). The politics of institutional renovation and economic upgrading: recombining the vines that bind in Argentina. *Politics & Society* 35(1), 103–144.

McGuire, James W. (2001). Social policy and mortality decline in East Asia and Latin America. *World Development* 29 (10), 1673–97.

    (2010). *Wealth, Health, and Democracy in East Asia and Latin America*. New York: Cambridge University Press.

Melo, Alberto, and Andres Rodriguez-Clare (2006). Productive development policies and supporting institutions in Latin America and the Caribbean. Inter-American Development Bank Working Paper C-106. Washington, DC: Inter-American Development Bank Research Department, Competitiveness Study Series.

Meyns, Peter, and Charity Musamba, eds. (2012). *The Developmental State in Africa: Problems and Prospects*. Duisburg, Essen: Institute for Development and Peace, INEF Report 101/2012.

Mkandawire, Thandika (2001). Thinking about developmental states in Africa. *Cambridge Journal of Economics* 25(3), 289–313.

(2017). State capacity, history, structure and political contestation in Africa. In Miguel Centeno, Atul Kohli, and Deborah Yashar with Dinish Mistree, eds., *States in the Developing World*. New York, NY: Cambridge University Press, pp. 184–216.

Moon, Chung-in, and Rashemi Prasad (1997). Beyond the developmental state: networks, politics and institutions. Governance 7(4): 360–386.

Naughton, Barry (2010). China's distinctive system: can it be a model for others? *Journal of Contemporary China* 19(65), 437–460.

Nelson, Richard R. (1993). *National Innovations Systems: A Comparative Perspective*. New York: Oxford Univesity Press.

Nelson, Richard R. and Sidney G. Winter (1983). *An Evolutionary Theory of Economic Change*. Cambridge: Harvard University Press.

Noble, Gregory (1998). *Collective Action in East Asia: How Ruling Parties Shape Industrial Policy*. Ithaca, NY: Cornell University Press.

Noland, Marcus, and Howard Pack (2003). *Industrial Policy in the an Era of Globalization*. Washington, DC: Institute for International Economics.

North, Douglass (1981). *Structure and Change in Economic History*. New York, NY: W. W. Norton.

(1990). *Institutions, Institutional Change and Economic Performance*. Cambridge: Cambridge University Press.

North, D., and R. Thomas (1973). *The Rise of the Western World: A New Economic History*. Cambridge: Cambridge University Press.

North, Douglas., John J. Wallis and Barry Weingast (2009). *Violence and Social Orders: A Conceptual Framework for Interpreting Recorded Human History*. New York: Cambridge University Press.

O'Donnell, Guillermo (1973). *Modernization and Bureaucratic-Authoritarianism: Studies in South American Politics*. Berkeley, CA: University of California, Institute of International Studies.

Okazaki, Tetsuji (1997). The government-firm relationship in postwar Japanese economic recovery: resolving the coordination failure by coordination in industrial rationalization. In Aoki, Masahiko, Hyung-Ki Kim, and Masahiro Okuno-Fujiwara, eds., *The Role of Government in East Asian Economic Development: Comparative Institutional Analysis*. New York, NY: Oxford University Press.

Okimoto, Daniel I. (1989). *Between MITI and the Market: Japanese Industrial Policy for High Technology*. Stanford, CA: Stanford University Press.

Okita, Saburo (1985). Special presentation: prospect of Pacific economies. *The Fourth Pacific Economic Cooperation Conference*. Seoul: Korea Development Institute, 18-29.

Olson, Mancur (1993). Dictatorship, democracy and development. *American Political Science Review* 87(3), 567-576.

Öniş, Ziya (1991). The logic of the developmental state. *Comparative Politics* 24(1), 109-126.

Ozawa, Terutomo (1993). Foreign direct investment and structural transformation: Japan as recycler of market and industry. *Business and the Contemporary World* 5, 129-150.

Pack, Howard (2001). Technological change and growth in East Asia: Macro and micro perspectives, in Joseph Stiglitz and Shahid Yusuf, eds. *Rethinking the East Asian Miracle*. New York: Oxford University Press.

Pack, Howard, and Kamal Saggi (2006). Is there a case for industrial policy? A critical survey. *The World Bank Research Observer* 21(2), 267-297.

Patrick, Hugh, and Henry Rosovsky, eds. (1976). *Asia's New Giant: How the Japanese Economy Works*. Washington, DC: The Brookings Institution.

Paus, Eva (2012a). Confronting the middle income trap: insights from small latecomers. *Studies in Comparative International Development* 47(2), 115-138.

(2012b). The rise and fall of the Celtic tiger: when deal-making trumps developmentalism. *Studies in Comparative International Development* 47(2), 161-184.

Pekannen, Saadia (2003). *Picking Winners? From Technology Catch-up to the Space Race in Japan*. Stanford, CA: Stanford University Press.

Pempel, T. J. (1978). Japanese foreign economic policy: the domestic bases for international behavior. In Peter Katzenstein, ed., *Between Power and Plenty: Foreign Economic Policies of Advanced Industrial States*. Madison, WI: University of Wisconsin Press.

Pempel, T. J., and Keiichi Tsunekawa (1979). Corporatism without labor: the Japanese anomaly. In Philippe Schmitter and Gerard Lembruch, eds., *Trends toward Corporatist Intermediation*. Beverly Hills, CA: Sage Publications.

Piore, Michael, and Charles Sable (1984). *The Second Industrial Divide: Possibilities for Prosperity*. New York, NY: Basic Books.

Pipkin, Seth and Alberto Fuentes (2017). Spurred to upgrade: A review of triggers and consequences of industrial upgrading in the global value chain literature. *World Development* 98 (10), 536-554.

Pollard, Sidney (1981). *Peaceful Conquest: The Industrialization of Europe 1760-1970.* New York, NY: Oxford University Press.

Prebisch, Raul (1950). *The Economic Development of Latin America and Its Principle Problems.* New York, NY: United Nations.

Pritchett, Lant, and Lawrence Summers (2014). Asiaphoria meets regression to the mean. NBER Working Paper 20573. Cambridge, MA: National Bureau of Economic Research.

Przeworski, Adam, Michael E. Alvarez, Jose Antonio Cheibub, and Fernando Lemongi (2000). *Democracy and Development: Political Institutions and Well-Being in the World, 1950-1990.* New York, NY: Cambridge University Press.

Rainer Kattel, Jan A. Kregel, and Erik S. Reinert, eds. (2009). *Ragnar Nurkse: Trade and Development.* London: Anthem Press.

Rajan, Raghuram, and Luigi Zingales (2004). *Saving Capitalism from the Capitalists: Unleashing the Power of Financial Markets to Create Wealth and Spread Opportunity.* Princeton, NJ: Princeton University Press.

Ramesh, M. 2004. *Social Policy in East and South East Asia: Education, Health, Housing and Income Maintenance.* New York: Routledge Curzon.

Ramesh, M. with Mukul G. Asher. 2000. *Welfare Capitalism in Southeast Asia: Social Security, Health and Education Policies.* New York: St. Martin's Press.

Ramo, Joshua Cooper (2004). *Beijing Consensus.* London: Foreign Policy Center.

Ramseyer, Frances McCall, and J. Mark Rosenbluth (1993). *Japan's Political Marketplace.* Cambridge, MA: Harvard University Press.

Ranis, Gustav, Frances Stewart and Alejandro Ramirez (2000). Economic growth and human development. *World Development*, 28 (2), 197-219.

Rasiah, Rajah (1994). Flexible production systems and local machine tool wubcontracting: Electronics component transnationals in Malaysia. *Cambridge Journal of Economics* 18 (3)3: 279-298.

(1995). *Foreign Capital and Industrialization in Malaysia.* New York: St Martin's.

(2001). Politics, institutions,. and flexibility: Microelectronics trans-
nationals and machine tool linkages in Malaysia in Frederic
C. Deyo, Richard F. Doner and Eric Hershberg, eds. *Economic
Governance and the Challenge of Flexibility in East Asia.* Oxford:
Rowman and Littlefield.

Reinert, Erik (2007). *How Rich Countries Got Rich and Why Poor Countries
Stay Poor.* New York, NY: PublicAffairs.

Rhee, Jong Chan. (1994). *The State and Industry in South Korea:
The Limits of the Authoritarian State.* New York: Routledge.

Riain, Sean O. (2014). Liberal globalization, capabilities, and the developmental network state in Ireland. In Michelle Williams, ed., *The End
of the Developmental State?* London: Routledge.

Robinson, Mark, and Gordon White, eds. (1998). *The Democratic
Developmental State.* Oxford: Oxford University Press.

Rock, Michael (2013). East Asia's democratic developmental states and
economic growth. *Journal of East Asian Studies* 13(1), 1–34.

Rodan, Garry (1989). *The Political Economy of Singapore's Industrialisation,*
London: Macmillan.

Rodriguez, Francisco, and Dani Rodrik (1999). Trade policy and eco-
nomic growth: a skeptic's guide to cross-national evidence. NBER
Working Paper No. W7081. Cambridge, MA: National Bureau for
Economic Research.

Rodrik, Dani. 1995. Getting interventions right: how South Korea and
Taiwan grew rich. *Economic Policy* 10(20), 53–107.

(2007). Normalizing industrial policy. Unpublished manuscript,
Harvard University, Kennedy School of Government.

(2008). *One Economics, Many Recipes: Globalization, Institutions, and
Economic Growth.* Princeton, NJ: Princeton University Press.

(2015). Premature deindustrialization. Unpublished ms., Kennedy
School of Government, Harvard University.

Romer, Paul M. (1986). Increasing returns and long-run growth. *Journal
of Political Economy* 94(5), 1002–1037.

Root, Hilton L. (1996). *Small Countries, Big Lessons: Governance and the
Rise of East Asia.* New York, NY: Oxford University Press.

Rosenstein-Rodan, Paul (1943). Problems of industrialization of
Eastern and South-Eastern Europe. *Economic Journal* 53(210/211),
202–211.

Rothstein, Bo, and Jan Teorell (2012). Defining and measuring quality
governance. In Soren Holmberg and Bo Rothstein, eds., *Good*

Government: The Relevance of Political Science. Cheltenham: Edward
    Elgar, pp. 13–39.
Routley, Laura (2012). Developmental states: a review of the literature.
    Effective States and Inclusive Development Working Paper No. 3.
    Manchester: ESID (February).
    (2014). Developmental states in Africa: a review of on-going debates
    and buzzwords. *Development Policy Review* 32(2), 159–177.
Sachs, Jefrey, and Andrew Warner (1995). Economic reform and the
    process of global integration. *Brookings Papers on Economic
    Activity* 1, 1–118.
Samuels, Richard J. (1987). *The Business of the Japanese State: Energy
    Markets in Comparative and Historical Perspective.* Ithaca, NY:
    Cornell University Press.
Sandbrook, Richard, Marc Edelman, Patrick Heller, and Judith Teichman
    (2007). *Social Democracy in the Global Periphery: Origins, Challenges,
    Prospects.* New York, NY: Cambridge University Press.
Saxenian, Annalee (1994). *Regional Advantage: Culture and Competition
    in Silicon Valley and Route 128.* Cambridge, MA: Harvard University
    Press.
Schein, H. Edgar (1997). *Strategic Pragmatism: The Culture of Singapore's
    Economic Development Board,* Cambridge, MA: MIT Press.
Schleifer, Andrei, and Robert W. Vishney (1993). Corruption. *Quarterly
    Journal of Economics* 108(3), 599–617.
Schmoller, Gustav (1884/1902). *The Mercantile System and Its Historical
    Significance.* New York, NY: Macmillan.
Schrank, Andrew (2011). Co-producing workplace transformation: the
    Dominican Republic in comparative perspective. *Socio-Economic
    Review* 9, 419–445.
Sen, Amartya (1999). *Development as Freedom.* New York, NY: Oxford
    University Press.
Singer, Hans (1950). The distribution of gains between investing and
    borrowing countries. *American Economic Review* 40(2), 473–485.
Singh, Ajit (1977). UK industry and the world economy: a case of
    deindustrialization? *Cambridge Journal of Economics* 1(2), 113–136.
    (1989). Third World competition and de-industrialization in advanced
    countries. *Cambridge Journal of Economics,* 13, 103–120.
Sohal, Amrik S., and Bill Ferme (1996). An analysis of the South Korean
    automotive, shipbuilding and steel industries. *Benchmarking:
    An International Journal* 3(2), 15–30.

Solow, Robert (1956). A contribution to the theory of economic growth, *The Quarterly Journal of Economics*, 70 (1), 65-94.

Srinivasan, T. N., and Jagdish Bhagwati (2001). Outward-orientation and development: are revisionists right? In Deepak Lal and Richard Snape, eds., *Trade, Development and Political Economy: Essays in Honor of Anne Krueger*. London: Palgrave, pp. 3-26.

Stern, Joseph J., Ji-hong Kim, Dwight Perkins, and Jung-ho Yoo (1995). *Industrializaiton and the State: The Korean Heavy and Chemical Industry Drive*. Cambridge, MA: Harvard Institute for International Development.

Stiglitz, Joseph (1996). Some lessons from the East Asian miracle. *World Bank Research Observer*. 11 (2): 151-178.

(2001). *Joseph Stiglitz and the World Bank: The Rebel Within*. Edited with commentary by Ha-Joon Chang. London: Anthem Press.

(2002). *Globalization and Its Discontents*. New York, NY: W. W. Norton.

Tan, Jeff (2014). Running out of steam? Manufacturing in Malaysia. *Cambridge Journal of Economics* 38, 153-180

Tilly, Charles (1985). War making and state making as organized crime. In Peter Evans, Dietrich Rueschemeyer, and Theda Skocpol, eds., *Bringing the State Back In*. New York, NY: Cambridge University Press.

Tyson, Laura D'Andrea (1993). *Who's Bashing Whom? Trade Conflict in High-Tech Industries*. Washington, DC: Institute for International Economics.

Veblen, Thorsten. 1915a. *Imperial Germany and the Industrial Revolution*. New York, NY: Macmillan.

1915b. The opportunity of Japan. *The Journal of Race Development* 6(1), 23-38

Vernon, Raymond. (1966). International investment and international trade in the product cycle. *Quarterly Journal of Economics* 80(2), 190-207.

Viner, Jacob (1948). Power versus plenty as objectives of foreign policy in the seventeenth and eighteenth centuries. *World Politics* 1(1), 1-29.

Vu, Tuong (2010). *Paths to Development in Asia: South Korea, Vietnam, China, and Indonesia*. New York: Cambridge University Press.

Wade, Robert (1990/2004). *Governing the Market: Economic Theory and the Role of Government in East Asian Industrialization*. Princeton, NJ: Princeton University Press.

(1996). Japan, the World Bank, and the art of paradigm maintenance: the East Asian miracle in political perspective. *New Left Review* 217, 3–36.

Wade, Robert, and Frank Veneroso (1998). The Asian crisis: the high debt model versus the Wall Street–Treasury–IMF Complex. *New Left Review* 228, 1–24.

Waldner, David (1999). *State-Building and Late Development*. Ithaca: Cornell University Press.

Weingast, Barry (1995). The economic role of political institutions. *Journal of Law, Economics, and Organization* 7, 1–31

(1997). The political foundations of democracy and the rule of law. *American Political Science Review* 91(2), 245–63.

Weiss, Linda (1998). *The Myth of the Powerless State: Governing the Economy in a Global Era*. Cambridge: Polity Press.

Weiss, Linda, and John Hobson (1995). *States and Economic Development: A Comparative Historical Analysis*. Cambridge: Polity Press.

White, Gordon (2006). Towards a democratic developmental state. *IDS Bulletin* 37(4), 60–70.

White, Gordon and Robert Wade (1984). Developmental States in East Asia, *special issue of* IDS Bulletin 15(2), 1–71.

Williams, Michelle, ed. (2014). *The End of the Developmental State?* London: Routledge.

Wong, Joseph (2004). The adaptive developmental state. *Journal of East Asian Studies* 4 (3), 345-362.

(2011) *Betting on Biotech Innovation and the Limits of Asia's Developmental State*. Ithaca: Cornell University Press.

Wong, Poh Kam (1994). Singapore's technology strategy. In Dennis. F. Simon, ed., *Emerging Technological Trajectory in the Pacific Rim*. Armonk, NY: M. E. Sharpe.

Wong, Poh Kam, and Chee-Yuen Ng, eds. (2001). *Industrial Policy, Innovation and Economic Growth: The Experience of Japan and the East Asian NIEs*, Singapore: Singapore University Press.

Woo, Jung-en (1991). *Race to the Swift: State and Finance in Korean Industrialization*. New York, NY: Columbia University Press.

Woo-Cumings, Meredith, ed. (1999). *The Developmental State*. Ithaca, NY: Cornell University Press.

Wood, Adrian (1994). *North-South Trade, Employment and Inequality: Changing Fortunes in a Skill-Driven World*. New York, NY: Oxford University Press.

The World Bank (1993). *The East Asian Miracle: Economic Growth and Public Policy*. New York, NY: Oxford University Press for the World Bank.

Yoffie, David (1983). *Power and Protectionism: Strategies of the Newly Industrializing Countries*. New York: Columbia University Press.

You, Jong-sung (2015). *Democracy, Inequality and Corruption: Korea, Taiwan and the Philippines Compared*. Cambridge: Cambridge University Press.

Young, Alywn (1992). Tale of two cities: factor accumulation and technical change in Hong Kong and Singapore. *NBER Macroeconomics Annual: 1992*. Cambridge, MA: MIT Press.

   1995. The Tyranny of Numbers: Confronting the Statistical Realities of the East Asian Growth Experience, *Quarterly Journal of Economics* 110, 641–680.

Yusuf, Shahid (2003). *Innovative East Asia: The Future of Growth*. Washington, DC: The World Bank.

Zhao, Suisheng (2017). Whither the China model: revisiting the debate. *Journal of Contemporary China* 26(103), 1–17.

Zysman, John (1984). *Governments, Markets and Growth: Financial Systems and Politics of Industrial Change*. Ithaca, NY: Cornell University Press.

Zysman, John, and Laura Tyson, eds. (1983). *American Industry in International Competition*. Ithaca, NY: Cornell University Press.

Printed in the United States
By Bookmasters